CANDIDE

CANDIDE

A COMIC OPERETTA BASED ON VOLTAIRE'S SATIRE

BOOK BY LILLIAN HELLMAN

SCORE BY LEONARD BERNSTEIN

LYRICS BY RICHARD WILBUR

Other lyrics by JOHN LATOUCHE and DOROTHY PARKER

RANDOM HOUSE, NEW YORK

For Tyrone Guthrie

CANDIDE *was first presented by Ethel Linder Reiner, in association with Lester Osterman, Jr., at the Martin Beck Theatre, New York City, on December 1, 1956, with the following cast:*

ACT ONE

SCENE I *Westphalia*

DR. PANGLOSS	Max Adrian
CUNEGONDE	Barbara Cook
CANDIDE	Robert Rounseville
BARON	Robert Mesrobian
MAXIMILLIAN	Louis Edmonds
KING OF HESSE	Conrad Bain
HESSE'S GENERAL	Norman Roland

SCENE IA *Candide Travels to Lisbon*

CANDIDE	Robert Rounseville
MAN	Boris Aplon
WOMAN	Doris Okerson
DUTCH LADY	Margaret Roy
DUTCH MAN	Tony Drake
ATHEIST	Robert Rue

SCENE 2 *Lisbon*

ARAB CONJUROR	Robert Barry
CANDIDE	Robert Rounseville
INFANT CASMIRA	Maria Novotna
DR. PANGLOSS	Max Adrian
LAWYER	William Chapman

VERY, VERY OLD INQUISITOR	Conrad Bain
VERY OLD INQUISITOR	Charles Aschmann

(Junkman, Robert Cosden; Wine-Seller, Stanley Grover; Bear, Charles Morrell; Bear Man, Robert Rue; Alchemist, Charles Aschmann; Grocery Lady, Margaret Roy.)

SCENE 2A *Candide Travels to Paris*

BEGGARS	Margaret Roy
	Robert Cosden
	Thomas Pyle
CANDIDE	Robert Rounseville
FRENCH LADY	Maud Scheerer

SCENE 3 *Paris*

OLD LADY	Irra Petina
MARQUIS MILTON	Boris Aplon
SULTAN MILTON	Joseph Bernard
CUNEGONDE	Barbara Cook
CANDIDE	Robert Rounseville
PILGRIM FATHER	Robert Rue

SCENE 3A *They Travel to Buenos Aires*

PILGRIM FATHER	Robert Rue
PILGRIM MOTHER	Dorothy Krebill
CUNEGONDE	Barbara Cook
OLD LADY	Irra Petina
CANDIDE	Robert Rounseville
CAPTAIN	Conrad Bain

SCENE 4 *Buenos Aires*

MARTIN	Max Adrian
CAPTAIN	Conrad Bain

PILGRIM FATHER	Robert Rue
CANDIDE	Robert Rounseville
CUNEGONDE	Barbara Cook
OLD LADY	Irra Petina
MAXIMILLIAN	Louis Edmonds
GOVERNOR OF BUENOS AIRES	William Olvis
OFFICERS	George Blackwell Tony Drake Thomas Pyle

ACT TWO

SCENE 1 *Buenos Aires*

CUNEGONDE	Barbara Cook
GOVERNOR OF BUENOS AIRES	William Olvis
OLD LADY	Irra Petina
MARTIN	Max Adrian
CANDIDE	Robert Rounseville
OFFICERS	George Blackwell Tony Drake Thomas Pyle

SCENE 1A *Candide Travels to Venice*

| CANDIDE | Robert Rounseville |
| MARTIN *and* DR. PANGLOSS | Max Adrian |

SCENE 2 *Venice*

FERONE	William Chapman
MADAME SOFRONIA	Irra Petina
DUCHESS	Maud Scheerer
PREFECT OF POLICE	Norman Roland
PRINCE IVAN (FAT MAN)	Robert Mesrobian
SCRUB LADY	Barbara Cook

CANDIDE	Robert Rounseville
DR. PANGLOSS	Max Adrian
SULTAN MILTON	Joseph Bernard
MARQUIS MILTON	Boris Aplon

(Duke of Naples, Charles Aschmann; Croupier, Robert Barry; Lady Cutely, Dori Davis; Lady Toothly, George Blackwell; Lady Soothly, Fred Jones; Lady Richmond, Thomas Pyle.)

Scene 3   *Westphalia*

MAXIMILLIAN	Louis Edmonds
CUNEGONDE	Barbara Cook
CANDIDE	Robert Rounseville
OLD LADY	Irra Petina
DR. PANGLOSS	Max Adrian

SINGERS: Peggyann Alderman, Charles Aschmann, Robert Barry, George Blackwell, Dori Davis, Jack DeLon, Tony Drake, Naomi Farr, Stanley Grover, Fred Jones, Mollie Knight, Dorothy Krebill, Vivian Laurence, Henry Lawrence, Robert Mesrobian, Lois Monroe, Doris Okerson, Thomas Pyle, Margaret Roy, Robert Rue, Mara Shorr, Dorothy White.

DANCERS: Alvin Beam, Charles Czarny, Marvin Gordon, Carmen Gutierrez, Charles Morrell, Frances Noble, Liane Plane, Gloria Stevens.

Directed by Tyrone Guthrie
Assisted by Tom Brown
Production designed by Oliver Smith
Costumes by Irene Sharaff
Lighting by Paul Morrison
Production Associate, Thomas Hammond
Musical Director, Samuel Krachmalnick
Orchestrations by Leonard Bernstein and Hershy Kay

MUSICAL NUMBERS

ACT ONE

SCENE 1

Ensemble: "The Best of All Possible Worlds" Pangloss and Chorus
Duet: "Oh, Happy We" Candide and Cunegonde
Song: "It Must Be So" Candide

SCENE 2

Lisbon Sequence Infant Casmira, Conjuror, and Chorus

SCENE 2A

Song: "It Must Be Me" Candide

SCENE 3

Mazurka
Aria: "Glitter and Be Gay" Cunegonde
Duet: "You Were Dead, You Know" Candide and Cunegonde

SCENE 3A

Pilgrims' Procession Pilgrims

SCENE 4

Serenade: "My Love" The Governor, Cunegonde, Old Lady
Tango: "I Am Easily Assimilated" Old Lady, Cunegonde and Chorus
Quartet Finale Cunegonde, Candide, Old Lady and Governor

Act Two

Scene 1

Trio: "Quiet"	Cunegonde, Old Lady and Governor
Ballad: "Eldorado"	Candide
Schottische: "Bon Voyage"	Governor and Chorus

Scene 2

Waltz: "What's the Use?"	Old Lady, Bazzini, Ferone, Ivan and Chorus
Gavotte	Pangloss, Old Lady, Cunegonde and Candide

Scene 3

Finale: "Make Our Garden Grow"	Entire Company

ACT ONE

ACT ONE

Scene I

The Scene: Westphalia. Outside the castle of the BARON THUN-
DER TEN TRONCH.
At rise: PANGLOSS *appears.*

PANGLOSS

I have been asked to tell you that this is Westphalia. It is a
fine, sunny day. The sun shines on all wedding days, except, of
course, when it doesn't, and then what does it matter? The
women of Westphalia are very pure women.

(*The* WOMEN *of the* CHORUS *appear*)

I am told there are women in this world who are not pure, but
the uneducated say a great many foolish things, don't they?
(*The* MEN *of the* CHORUS *appear*) Our men are brave. The
war is over, but we still have six divisions of artillery.

It's been a long and bloody war, but if men didn't fight they
would never know the benefits of peace, and if they didn't know
the benefits of peace they would never know the benefits of war.
You see, it all works out for the best.

(KING OF HESSE, *escorted by soldiers, appears*)

This is the King of Hesse, our hereditary enemy. We destroyed his army last week and took him prisoner. We treat him
with great courtesy. He has a nice room in the basement. He
comes out every day for exercise, and seems most content.

(HESSE *exits*)

3

Oh, forgive me. I am Pangloss, Doctor of Heidelberg, of Leipzig, and of Würzburg, in Philosophy and Metaphysics. I have long been resident tutor to the Baron's house. It's been a good life. Although, between you and me, I sometimes miss the cloisters of the university and small talk in Greek.

(GRETCHEN *comes toward him*)
Good morning, Gretchen.

GRETCHEN

You owe me money.

PANGLOSS

Ah, well. If she didn't think of money, she wouldn't think at all. Which certainly proves that all is for the best in this best of all possible worlds.

(*He sings*)
Look at this view! Mountains and towers!
Green meadows, too, bursting with flowers!
This is the heart of the best of all possible worlds.
Much the best part of the best of all possible worlds.

(CHORUS *sings*)
Yes, it's the heart of the best of all possible worlds.
Much the best part of the best of all possible worlds.

(PANGLOSS *sings, gesturing toward the* CHORUS)
Our men are lean, handsome and active.
Where have you seen girls more attractive?
None have more grace in this best of all possible worlds.
No finer race in this best of all possible worlds.

4

(CHORUS *sings*)
No finer race in this best of all possible worlds.
No better place in this best of all possible worlds.

(PANGLOSS *sings*)
And best of all, we now convene
With keen anticipation,
To watch a happy wedding scene
And have a celebration.

(CHORUS *sings*)
A happy celebration.

(PANGLOSS *sings*)
All hail the groom
And bride, of whom
Our hearts could not be fonder.
The love that reigns in Heaven above
Is mirrored in the marriage of
(CANDIDE *and* CUNEGONDE *enter.* PANGLOSS *continues sing-
ing*)
Candide and Cunegonde!

(CHORUS *sings*)
Candide and Cunegonde!

(PANGLOSS *sings*)
Wherefore and hence, therefore and ergo—

(CHORUS *sings*)
Wherefore and hence, therefore and ergo—

(PANGLOSS *sings*)

All's for the best in this best of all possible worlds.

(CHORUS *sings*)

All's for the best in this best of all possible worlds.

(PANGLOSS *sings*)

Any questions?
Ask without fear.
    (*Touches his head*)
I've all the answers here.

(CUNEGONDE *sings*)

Dear master, I am sure you're right
That married life is splendid.
But why do married people fight?
I cannot comprehend it.

(CHORUS *sings*)

She cannot comprehend it.

(PANGLOSS *sings*)

The private strife
Of man and wife
Is useful to the nation:
It is a harmless outlet for
Emotions which could lead to war
Or social agitation.

(CHORUS *sings*)

A brilliant explanation!

(PANGLOSS *sings*)
Therefore, it's true.
No one may doubt it:

(CHORUS *sings*)
Therefore, it's true.
No doubt about it:

(PANGLOSS *sings*)
Marriage is blest in
This best of all possible worlds.

(CHORUS *sings*)
All's for the best in
This best of all possible worlds.

(PANGLOSS *sings*)
Next question?
Deep though it be,
There's none too deep for me!

(CANDIDE *sings*)
Since marriage is divine, of course,
We cannot understand, sir,
Why should there be so much divorce.
Do let us know the answer.

(CHORUS *sings*)
Do let us know the answer.

(PANGLOSS *sings*)
Why, marriage, boy,
Is such a joy,

So lovely a condition,
That many ask no better than
To wed as often as they can,
In happy repetition.

(CHORUS *sings*)
A brilliant exposition!

(PANGLOSS, CANDIDE, CUNEGONDE *sing*)
Wherefore and hence, therefore and ergo....

(CHORUS *sings*)
Wherefore and hence, therefore and ergo....

(PANGLOSS *sings*)
All's for the best in this best of all possible worlds.

(CHORUS *sings*)
All's for the best in this best of all possible worlds.

(PANGLOSS, CUNEGONDE, CANDIDE *sing*)
A brilliant exposition!
Q.E.D.
All's for the best.

(ALL *sing*)
A brilliant exposition in this best of all
Possible, possible, possible, possible worlds!
A brilliant exposition! Q.E.D.
(*The* BARON THUNDER TEN TRONCH *enters.*)

CANDIDE

CUNEGONDE

(Speaks)

Good morning, dear Father.

BARON

A good morning, dear children, on your wedding day.
(MAXIMILLIAN *enters. He is hung with medals*) Good morning, son. Where did you get the medals?

MAXIMILLIAN

Oh, now, Father, I have one of my headaches.

BARON

Have you had a headache for three years? Why didn't you
join the army when I sent for you? (*Points to* CANDIDE) My
adopted son never left my side. He earned his medals.

MAXIMILLIAN

I sprained my ankle, Father. I have soft bones. I've explained
it all before—

BARON

Candide didn't worry about his bones. He worried about
mine.

MAXIMILLIAN

He has strong bones. Lower-class bones.

PANGLOSS

Baron, here are the marriage contracts in Latin, Greek and
Westphalian dialect. A record for history.

9

CANDIDE

MAXIMILLIAN

(*To* CUNEGONDE)

As your brother—and the future head of this house, God forbid Father ever dies—I must once again protest your marriage to a man of unknown birth. And if you hadn't paid so much for your wedding dress, I could have had a new uniform.

CUNEGONDE

(*Laughs*)

But it's a nice uniform. And certainly not touched by war.

BARON

(*To* CANDIDE)

Come sign the marriage contracts, my boy.

CANDIDE

(*Coming to table*)

Oh, sir, I can make no marriage settlement. You know I have nothing to give Cunegonde.

PANGLOSS

You have a pure heart. A woman wants nothing else.

CANDIDE

(*To* BARON)

You have been much too generous with Cunegonde's dowry. I cannot accept—

10

BARON

I haven't given her a damn thing.

CANDIDE

Thank you, sir. Thank you. And now I have a great favor to ask of you—

BARON

(*Very quickly*)

I can't afford anything. I must look out for my old age. What is it?

CANDIDE

This is the happiest day of my life and it pains me to think we have a prisoner in the house. Could we invite the King of Hesse to have wine and cake with us at the marriage feast?

(BARON *nods, signals to a soldier. The soldier exits to fetch the* KING OF HESSE.)

PANGLOSS

(*To* CANDIDE, *as they move away*)

Your old teacher is proud of you. Now make me happy. Throw yourself back through the years and repeat your lesson: tell me the golden rules of a high-minded Wesphalian man.

CANDIDE

The heart of mankind is a generous heart; the honor of a man is all he needs on life's journey; the poor must be respected and so must the rich since they are always with us; the beauty of noble thought; the treasure that is sweet, sacred womanhood—

PANGLOSS

(*To a pretty girl who passes*)

Good morning, Paquette.

PAQUETTE

You owe me money.

PANGLOSS

(*To* CANDIDE)

Women are sometimes difficult. But if they weren't difficult perhaps nobody would pay any attention to them. Tell me, my boy, do you know much of women? Have you, I mean did you, perhaps, in a daring minute—

CANDIDE

What, sir? I don't know what you mean.

PANGLOSS

(*Delighted*)

Oh, I am so glad. So glad. (*To another pretty girl*) Hello, Irmentrude. You look charming—(*Quickly*) I paid you.
(*She disappears.*)

PANGLOSS

(*Hurries to* CUNEGONDE)

Cunegonde, my dear little girl, make your old teacher happy. Repeat the words of a high-minded Westphalian lady and swear that you will live by them.

CUNEGONDE

The honor of a woman is all she needs on life's journey. Dr. Pangloss, is that really all a woman needs?

PANGLOSS

Nothing else.

CUNEGONDE

Yes, sir. Do you like my dress?

PANGLOSS

Continue, dear girl: The treasure that is sweet, sacred womanhood—

CUNEGONDE

Treasure. Yes, sir. Do you think it will rain? If it rains, my hair won't curl—(*Pats* PANGLOSS *affectionately*) I'm a bad pupil. I always was. But don't be angry with me.
(PANGLOSS *smiles, kisses her, and moves to* MAXIMILLIAN.)

PANGLOSS

Maximillian, I have a new medal for you. Come along.
(*They exit.*)

BARON

(*To* CUNEGONDE)
And how's my pretty daughter? Nervous as a bride should be?

CUNEGONDE

No, Father. I am not nervous.

BARON
(*As he exits*)
Oh, my God. Neither was your mother.

CANDIDE

We're alone. We shouldn't be.

CUNEGONDE

Why not? What silly old customs. We'll be married in a few
minutes. Would you like to see my veil?
(*She moves toward him. He draws back.*)

CANDIDE

Cunegonde, you know that I am forbidden to see the wedding
veil—

CUNEGONDE

For a daring hero, you're not very daring.

CANDIDE

I respect you and I—

CUNEGONDE
(*Too firmly*)
You should respect me. I'm very pure.

CANDIDE

You need hardly tell me such a thing.

CUNEGONDE

I've never even thought about another man. I've never kissed
another man.

14

CANDIDE

(*Amazed*)

Of course not, Cunegonde.

CUNEGONDE

I think you should apologize, darling.

CANDIDE

I do. (*Bewildered*) Indeed I do.

CUNEGONDE

All right. I forgive. Now where are we going on our honey-moon?

CANDIDE

Well, we'll stay here and take a nice picnic basket—(*Sadly*) I can't take you anywhere, Cunegonde. You know I have nothing.

CUNEGONDE

I don't want anything, darling. And anyway, Father's rich.

CANDIDE

I won't take anything from your father. (*Desperately*) Cunegonde, I will work for you, I will give my life for you, but that isn't much to offer. I can't even give you a house of your own—

CUNEGONDE

Darling, darling. We've said all this before. I don't want houses or dresses or jewelry—they're all rather vulgar, aren't

15

they? I'll live in this dress the rest of my life. These shoes will last me until death. I want nothing. Absolutely nothing but you.

(CANDIDE *sings*)
Soon, when we feel we can afford it,
We'll build a modest little farm.

(CUNEGONDE *sings*)
We'll buy a yacht and live aboard it,
Rolling in luxury and stylish charm.

(CANDIDE)
Cows and chickens.

(CUNEGONDE)
Social whirls.

(CANDIDE)
Peas and cabbage.

(CUNEGONDE)
Ropes of pearls.

(CANDIDE)
Soon there'll be little ones beside us;
We'll have a sweet Westphalian home.

(CUNEGONDE)
Somehow we'll grow as rich as Midas;
We'll live in Paris when we're not in Rome.

(CANDIDE)

Smiling babies.

(CUNEGONDE)

Marble halls.

(CANDIDE)

Sunday picnics.

(CUNEGONDE)

Costume balls.

(CUNEGONDE)

Oh, won't my robes of silk and satin
Be chic! I'll have all that I desire.

(CANDIDE)

Pangloss will tutor us in Latin
And Greek, while we sit before the fire.

(CUNEGONDE)

Glowing rubies.

(CANDIDE)

Glowing logs.

(CUNEGONDE)

Faithful servants.

(CANDIDE)

Faithful dogs.

(CUNEGONDE)

We'll round the world enjoying high life;
All will be pink champagne and gold.

(CANDIDE)

We'll lead a rustic and a shy life,
Feeding the pigs and sweetly growing old.

(CUNEGONDE)

Breast of peacock.

(CANDIDE)

Apple pie.

(CUNEGONDE)

I love marriage.

(CANDIDE)

So do I.

(CUNEGONDE)

Oh happy pair!
Oh, happy we!
It's very rare
How we agree.

(BOTH)

Oh happy pair!
Oh, happy we!
It's very rare
How we agree.

Oh happy pair!
Oh, happy we!
It's very rare
How we agree!
> (*The people of the scene return to the stage.*)

CANDIDE
> (*Moves to the* KING OF HESSE)

I would like to make you welcome at my wedding feast. Can you forget old battles on this happy day?

HESSE

I am happy to forget old battles. I don't like battles. I hate war.
> (*They shake hands and* CANDIDE *moves away. The* GEN-ERAL *of the Hessian army appears, hiding behind a pillar, and taps* HESSE *on the shoulder.*)

HESSE'S GENERAL
> (*In a whisper*)

Your Majesty.

HESSE

Oh, my God, what are you doing here?

HESSE'S GENERAL

Your Majesty, precisely at noon you will be rescued.

HESSE

I don't want to be rescued. I don't want to go home. I like being a prisoner. Go away, please.

We will not pay your ransom. We have been in conference all night and have decided it is cheaper to fight.

Please leave me alone. I'm sick of war—

The honor of Hesse calls for the destruction of Westphalia. Have a little honor, Your Majesty.

(*He creeps off.*)

We shall now sing the first eighteen stanzas of the wedding chorale, omitting the eleventh, twelfth and thirteenth stanzas which have to do with fertility festivals. We shall use the St. Stanislaus version.

(CHORUS *sings*)
We subjects of this Barony
Are gathered here in pride and glee
To hail the lovely bride-to-be
And graft upon her noble tree
The flower of chivalry.

(*The* GENERAL *of the Hessian army appears, signaling to his men. They invade Westphalia. Through the noise of battle, we hear the cries of Westphalian ladies, the outraged shouts of Westphalian men. We see* CUNEGONDE *carried off by the* GENERAL *as* CANDIDE *rushes to her defense. Ladies rush across the stage in panic as Hessian soldiers pursue them. In the midst of the excitement,* PANGLOSS *climbs on the wedding table.*)

PANGLOSS

Gentlemen! Gentlemen! I have never before in my life used strong words, but I am forced to say this is unsporting.
(*He is knocked off the table and disappears.*)

(*The last figures in the battle disappear. The stage is empty. After a second, the* BARON *and* MAXIMILLIAN *appear, struggle toward each other, and fall to the ground.* CUNEGONDE, *without her wedding dress, appears and falls to the ground trying to reach her father.* PANGLOSS *appears and struggles to reach the three figures.*)

PANGLOSS

Tut, tut, the good Baron. Tut, tut, the good Maximillian.
(*He moves toward* CUNEGONDE.)

PANGLOSS

Cunegonde. Cunegonde. Poor, pretty child.
(*He falls as* CANDIDE *comes stumbling on.*)

CANDIDE
(*Calling*)

Cunegonde, Cunegonde—

PANGLOSS

Candide—(CANDIDE *runs to him*) Cunegonde is dead. Westphalia is destroyed. Don't cry, don't stay to mourn us. The world is beautiful—go forth and see it.

CANDIDE

My Cunegonde—

PANGLOSS

Yes, I know. But think of it this way: If she hadn't died she'd never have been born. There is some sweetness in every woe. The world will be good to you, kind to you. Go now.

(*Music begins.* CANDIDE *moves slowly out of Westphalia.*)

Scene 1A

The Scene: Travels from Westphalia to Lisbon. The frame of a house is rolled on stage.

At rise: A woman and a man are sitting at a table, eating their large dinner and throwing away the food that does not please them.

CANDIDE
(*To the man and the woman*)
Please, have you any work for me? (*No answer*) I have traveled a long way. Could I rest in your stables?

MAN
No.

CANDIDE
Could I have a little of your garbage?

WOMAN
Certainly not.

(*The house rolls off stage.* CANDIDE *sings*)
My world is dust now,
And all I loved is dead.
Oh, let me trust now
In what my master said:
"There is a sweetness in every woe."
It must be so. It must be so.

The dawn will find me
Alone in some strange land.
But men are kindly;
They'll give a helping hand.
So said my master, and he must know.
It must be so. It must be so.

> (*The frame of three houses is wheeled on stage.* CANDIDE *knocks on first door. A woman appears.*)

CANDIDE

Bread, Ma'am?

> (*She shuts the door. He knocks on second door. A man appears*)

A little water, sir?

> (*The man makes an angry gesture.* CANDIDE *moves on to third door. A man hands him a loaf of bread.* CANDIDE *stares at the bread, unbelieving*)

Thank you, sir. You are a Christian.

MAN

How dare you? I am an atheist.

CANDIDE

I don't know what that is.

MAN

Never mind. Go your way. God bless you.

(CANDIDE *moves away as the market square of Lisbon is wheeled on stage.*)

The Scene: Lisbon. The market square. The day of the famous earthquake.

At rise: The sound of morning church bells. The INFANT CASMIRA, *her cage covered, is watched over by the* ARAB, *who is eating his breakfast. The booth keepers are eating their breakfast, getting ready for the crowd. During the following scene the stage will fill with people.*

CANDIDE *comes wandering on, staring at those who are eating. He does not see* PANGLOSS, *who, in beggar's rags, is sitting in a corner.*

BOOTH KEEPER
(*To* CANDIDE)
Fresh sausage? Breakfast coffee? Cheese?

CANDIDE
(*Touches sausage*)
Looks nice.

BOOTH KEEPER
Is nice. Three real.

CANDIDE
(*Shakes his head*)
I have no money. Where am I?

BOOTH KEEPER
I don't know where you are. I'm in Lisbon.

ARAB

(*As* CANDIDE *passes* INFANT'S *cage*)

Fortune told by wonderful child?

CANDIDE

No, thank you.

ARAB

You got heavy accent.

CANDIDE

So have you.
>   (*An arm comes out of cage, grabs* CANDIDE. *As he is pulled down, he is able to see into cage. He cries out in fear.*)

ARAB

She don't like you. She say you go away.

CANDIDE

(*Horrified*)

She? Is it a woman?
>   (INFANT *growls.*)

ARAB

The Infant Casmira is child. Imported greatest fortuneteller in Europe. (ARAB *leans down to listen to angry sounds from* INFANT) Go away, she say. She don't like you. She say you are force for good: a good little foolish man. Worries her. She say you make her angry. You be careful. Move.

(CANDIDE *moves on to bear and* BEAR KEEPER. *He stands watching them eat breakfast. The bear breaks off a piece of his meat and throws it to* CANDIDE.)

CANDIDE

(*Touched*)

Thank you. Thank you very much.

BEAR KEEPER

(*To bear*)

Damn old soft-hearted fool. (*To* CANDIDE) Move on. We don't like foreigners.

(*The* BEAR KEEPER *shoves* CANDIDE *into* PANGLOSS.)

CANDIDE

Nobody likes me.

PANGLOSS

Is that any reason for falling on my poor head? When I was young we did not kick philosophers.

CANDIDE

Excuse me, sir. I stumbled.

PANGLOSS

And if you had not stumbled, I would not have this bruise on my head. And if I did not have this bruise on my head, I would no longer know that I had a head, so weak am I from hunger.

CANDIDE

And I kicked you because I am weak from hunger. The weak kick the weak. That's sad, isn't it?

PANGLOSS

Not at all. If the weak didn't kick the weak, then the strong would kick the weak, and certainly that would hurt far more. You understand?

CANDIDE

No, sir.

PANGLOSS

Obviously, you are not equipped to think. Therefore, leave the thinking to wise men, and paste upon your heart this motto: All is for the best in this best of all possible worlds.

CANDIDE

It cannot be. It cannot be. What is your name? Who are you? (*The bundle of rags looks at him*) Pangloss! Dear master!

PANGLOSS

Candide. My boy, my boy ...
    (*They fall into each other's arms, crying.*)

CANDIDE

But I thought you were dead.

PANGLOSS

Yes, I thought I was dead. But a few hours after my death, I awoke unharmed. There was not a stone left in the castle, not a tree left standing. The Baron was dead, Maximillian was dead, Cunegonde was dead. . . . (CANDIDE *buries his head*) I know.

28

But you must be brave. It is a great thing that we have found each other again, happy and well....

CANDIDE

But, dear sir, you are not looking well. You must have been wounded during the battle of Westphalia....

PANGLOSS

No. I fainted during the battle. I don't like battles. You will remember that I believe intellectuals should fight only among themselves. How have you fared in the great, kind world, my dear boy?

CANDIDE

Badly, sir. The great, kind world is a cold place.

PANGLOSS

It pains me to hear you speak that way.

CANDIDE

I have seen the death of the woman I love, the destruction of my home and my friends. And along this miserable journey I have known little charity. I have begun to have doubts....

PANGLOSS

Doubt, my boy, is a word like death. Once a man begins to doubt, he begins to think for himself and upsets his stomach.

CANDIDE

My stomach is not upset...it's empty.

PANGLOSS

The emptier the stomach, the more power in the brain. Starved, I am at my very best....

(*He stumbles and falls as the market people begin to sing.*)

(TWO GIRLS *sing*)
Look at this, look at that.

(FIRST GIRL)
What a pretty new hat!

(SECOND GIRL)
But the price is much too high.

(WINE MERCHANT)
Here be wine!

(SPICE MERCHANT)
Here be spice!

(BOTH)
Worth at least twice the price.

(TWO GIRLS)
But we haven't any money
So there's nothing we can buy!

(ALL MEN)
Hurry hurry hurry,
Come and buy!

(ALL LADIES)

Hurry hurry hurry
Come and try!

(BEAR KEEPER)

See the great Russian bear!

(COSMETIC MERCHANT)

Buy a comb for your hair!

(LADIES)

But the price is much too high.

(DOCTOR)

Here be potions and pills
For your fevers and chills!

(LADIES)

But we haven't any money
So there's nothing we can buy!

(JUNKMAN)

Any kind of metal
Any kind of metal
Any kind of metal
Bought and sold!

(ALCHEMIST)

Any kind of metal
Any kind of metal
Any kind of metal
Turned to gold!

(BOTH)

Pots and pans,
Metal cans,

(JUNKMAN)

Bought or traded or sold!

(ALCHEMIST)

I can turn them into gold!

(BOTH)

Pans and pots and what-nots

(JUNKMAN)

Trading new ones for old!

(ALCHEMIST)

For a tiny fee my alchemy
Can turn them into gold!

(ALL *sing, in canon*)

Hurry hurry hurry,
Come and buy!
Hurry hurry hurry,
Come and try!
What a fair, what a fair!
Things to buy everywhere,
But the prices are too high!
It's not fair, it's not fair,
Things to buy everywhere;
But we haven't any money
So there's nothing we can buy!

ARAB

(*Calls out*)

AAAAAAAYYYYYYY have an announcement! Come look
on the Infant Casmira.

(CROWD *stops singing, moves toward him. In the cage we
see the* INFANT CASMIRA. *She is very small and is dressed
in child's costume. But she is not a child and she* is
drunk.)

(ARAB *sings*)

Deep in a trance that has lasted for three days.

Only six years old, she has powers to see underground.

Though she don't speak no language, she'll tell you the future,

She never has made a mistake; and all for

Two real, two shilling, two kopek, two lira.

Awaken her with the sound of silver.

(CROWD *throws coins. The* INFANT CASMIRA *begins to whirl
about.*)

(CROWD *sings*)

Is that a child?

She's rather wild to be a child!

(INFANT CASMIRA *sings*)

Ha ha ha ha

Ha ha ha ha ha ha

Ha ha ha ha

Ha ha ha ha ha ha!

(CROWD *sings*)

What does she say?

What does she say?

What does she say?

(INFANT CASMIRA *sings*)

Ho ho ho ho
Ho ho ho ho ho ho
Ho ho ho ho
Ho ho ho ho ho ho ho!

(ARAB *sings*)

She say:
There is terrible trouble.
Pretty soon there is gonna be terrible trouble.
Ay ay ay, such a terrible trouble.
Ay ay ay ay!

(CROWD *sings*)

What can it be?
What can it be?
What can it be?

(ARAB *sings*)

She say:
She cannot see the trouble
Because her eyesight is not enough clearly.
The only cure is to place two gold coins on her eyelids.
(*Somebody in* CROWD *throws coins*)
T'ank you. Now she will tell.

(INFANT *sings*)

I say: spirit voices have spoken.
They say that the ground gonna open.
That the earth gonna open and swallow the city of Lisbon

34

(CHORUS *sings*)

Ha, ha, ha—
The little fake.
    (*The earth does shake and the* CROWD *draws back in fear.*)

(INFANT *sings*)

The towers of Lisbon are trembling
I say the sky will be covered with dark wings
I say the sea will turn to blood
The earth will rise, shake, heave, roar—listen . . .

(INFANT *and* ARAB *sing*)

Fly!
Fly from the city of Lisbon
Fly from the city of Lisbon! Fly!

(CHORUS *sings*)

Oh, oh
Oh, oh

Simultaneously

(CHORUS *sings*)

Pray for us, pray for us
Fons pietatis,
Pray for us!
Davidis turris,
Pray for us!

Rex majestatis,
Pray for us!
Davidis turris,
Pray for us!

35

(*The* CROWD *panics*)

Pray for us, pray for us!
Fons pietatis,
Pray for us!
Davidis turris,
Pray for us!

Rex majestatis,
Pray for us!
Davidis turris,
Pray for us!

Fons pietatis,
Pray for us!
Davidis turris,
Pray for us!

Rex majestatis,
Pray for us!
Pray for us!
Pray for us!
(*Fanfare.*)

(*Two very old men, in thronelike chairs, are wheeled on. They are followed by a brisk young man in legal robes.*)

CANDIDE

(*To* PANGLOSS)

What is happening?

PANGLOSS

The Inquisition, assisted by great lawyers from the university.

CANDIDE

What is an inquisition?

PANGLOSS

(*Points to old men*)

A group of wise men who settle public problems with justice to all. It will be a pleasure to watch them.

LAWYER

(*To* CROWD)

The earth has shaken. Be calm. We have come to settle the shaking of the earth. Put your faith in these wise men. They, and they alone, know the cause. They, and they alone, will banish the danger. What causes the earth to tremble, sires?

VERY, VERY OLD INQUISITOR

Witches and wizards have moved among you. Send them forth for judgment.

VERY OLD INQUISITOR

(*Yawns*)

The witch and wizard stuff again?

LAWYER

(*To* CROWD)

Search among yourselves. Send forth the sinful. One gold piece for a witch. Two for a wizard. And ten more for the brave men who come forward with information.

(INFANT *is pushed forward by* ARAB.)

LAWYER

(*To* INFANT)

You confess to being a witch?

INFANT

(*Very drunk now*)

No, sir. I am a little child. (VERY, VERY OLD INQUISITOR, *frightened, tries to get off throne*) But I can point out the wizard. (*She points to* CANDIDE) He creep here this morning. In his bag he carry earthquake germs. You open bag and you find germs. He bring the danger. (*The police grab* CANDIDE. *They push him forward, open his bag. In the meantime,* ARAB *and* INFANT *advance to* LAWYER) Money, please.

LAWYER

It will be sent you.

(*He motions to police. They grab the* INFANT *and the* ARAB *and haul them off.*)

POLICEMAN

(*Who has been looking in* CANDIDE's *bag*)

Yes, sir. Germs of earthquake have been found.

LAWYER

(*To* CANDIDE)

You are charged with communication with the Devil.

VERY OLD INQUISITOR

Oh, come on. You always take too long. Guilty.

LAWYER

Just a minute, sir. We must observe certain legal, civil and moral laws as written into the code of Western liberalism. (*To* CANDIDE) Death by hanging.

PANGLOSS

(Pleasant, undisturbed, he comes forward)
Certainly, sirs, this is a most interesting entertainment. However, things must not go too far. How do you do. (*To* VERY, VERY OLD INQUISITOR) Haven't we met before? Did you have a brother at Heidelberg?

LAWYER

Who are you?
(PANGLOSS *hands him his papers.*)

PANGLOSS

(*To* VERY, VERY OLD INQUISITOR)
Could we dine together and, as educated men, tweak the tail of the cosmos over a bottle of cold wine?

LAWYER

These papers are in order. This man is a spy.
(PANGLOSS *is grabbed by the police.*)

CANDIDE

I don't understand any of this, good sirs. But Professor Pangloss is a great scholar. A believer in ... well ... in many, many things....

39

LAWYER

And do you believe in many, many things?

CANDIDE

No, sir, I have no beliefs.

PANGLOSS

No. Tell them what you do believe. Tell them the rules of a high-minded Westphalian man. Speak up, my boy.

CANDIDE

I believe that the heart of mankind is a generous heart. The honor of a man is all he needs on life's journey—

VERY OLD INQUISITOR

Guilty. Take them away.
(*The police grab them.*)

PANGLOSS

Gentlemen, this joke is becoming oppressive. It is necessary to understand the scientific fact that if the earth did not quake from time to time, man would grow too confident of his sense of balance, and if man becomes too confident of his sense of balance he will forget how to fall without injury to his head bones. I will be happy to share with you all German scientific knowledge—

VERY, VERY OLD INQUISITOR

We condemn you to death.

PANGLOSS

Oh, you have a right to your opinion, sir. But that's a rather important opinion. Why do you disapprove of me?

VERY, VERY OLD INQUISITOR

You're a foreigner. You're a bore. You're a German scientist. You're a danger. Take him off.

CANDIDE

But we have done nothing.

VERY, VERY OLD INQUISITOR

That's the hardest way to die. The guilty die easier than the innocent. They have a normal sense of accomplishment. Take them away.

(CANDIDE *and* PANGLOSS, *bewildered, are made ready for the hanging.*)

VERY OLD INQUISITOR

(*Addressing* CROWD)

I declare now an hour of private mourning and meditation. Go and gather the proper donations.

VERY, VERY OLD INQUISITOR

In gold. All donations are tax-deductible.

VERY OLD INQUISITOR

See to it that you fast until dinnertime.

VERY, VERY OLD INQUISITOR

And remember to give thanks that you have been saved from an earthquake. The danger is over.

(*The earth quakes. People are thrown to the ground, the buildings rock back and forth, and all is darkness. The earthquake is over. In the dim light we see* PAN-GLOSS. *He is on the gibbet, a rope around his neck.*)

PANGLOSS

Candide . . . The world is beautiful, my son. Go forth and see it. There is some sweetness in every woe.

(*He falls on the gibbet as the scene blacks out.*)

Scene 2A

The Scene: Travels from Lisbon to Paris.

(CANDIDE *appears, singing to himself, quietly and simply*)
My master told me
That men are loving-kind;
Yet now behold me
Ill-used and sad of mind.
Men must have kindness I cannot see.
It must be me. It must be me.

My master told me
The world is warm and good;
It deals more coldly
Than I had dreamt it would.
There must be sunlight I cannot see.
It must be me. It must be me.
(*He moves across stage toward a group of* BEGGARS. *The* BEGGARS *stare at him.*)

FIRST BEGGAR

You didn't sound like a beggar coming down the road. Better learn to walk slower, boy, and save your feet.

CANDIDE

I'm not a beggar.

SECOND BEGGAR

You're a king?

FIRST BEGGAR

I don't think he's a king.

THIRD BEGGAR

You're a general?

FIRST BEGGAR

I don't think he's a general.

CANDIDE

I was a soldier—

THIRD BEGGAR

You don't look it.

CANDIDE
(*With pain*)

I am not a beggar.

FIRST BEGGAR
(*Gets up*)

Let's move on to Paris: it's the beggar's city. There's always a party in Paris. (*They start off.* CANDIDE *does not move. The* FIRST BEGGAR *turns to* CANDIDE) Want to come with us, *soldier?*

(*They move off. Slowly* CANDIDE *follows them. The frame of a house is rolled on. A painted, elderly lady is standing in the window.*)

LADY

Bon soir, monsieur. You are bemused with wine?

CANDIDE

Oh, no, sir. I am bemused with weariness.

LADY

I am not a sir. I am a madame.

CANDIDE

Please excuse me. My head goes about from hunger.

LADY

Come in. Do. Cleaned, you would be handsome. At six o'clock, of course, you must disappear. My lover is very jealous....

CANDIDE

Your lover? I am indeed in Paris.

LADY

The outskirts of Paris.

(*The lights fade and come up on the ballroom of a fine Paris house.*)

SCENE 3

The Scene: Paris. The ballroom of a house in Paris. The garden can be seen. Left stage, a group of screens form a boudoir. At rise: The guests are waltzing about. Outside, in the garden, the BEGGARS *and* CANDIDE *are staring at the party.*

A MAN

(*To his partner*)

Who is giving this party?

HIS PARTNER

Two rich gentlemen. To introduce their niece, as one calls such women this year.

THE MAN

What's their names?

ANOTHER MAN

The Marquis something and the Sultan something. What difference does it make? The wine is good.

(*An* OLD LADY, *dressed to the nines, carrying something high above her head, comes dodging and tripping and falling among the dancers. She is followed by two eager gentlemen, the* MARQUIS *and the* SULTAN.)

MARQUIS

(*Nervous, to the* OLD LADY)

But where is she, where is madame? The guests have been waiting for an hour.

46

OLD LADY

(*Giggling*)

She didn't have the proper garters. We had to send to the jeweler.... (*Coquettishly opens the box*) Would it please you both to have a little, little look?

MARQUIS

Oh, yes!

SULTAN

It would please me to have a look at the lady.

OLD LADY

Oh, be patient, dear. It's her first Paris party, and she is nervous. How well I remember my first Paris party. Not like this, I can tell you. You had to present proof of seven titled ancestors at the door. That was the night the Duke of Hamburg saw me and killed himself. . . .

SULTAN

All right. So all right, already. (*Moves toward boudoir*) I'm going in.

OLD LADY

(*Hastily*)

Be patient. This girl has come from the cloisters, pure and innocent. You've been very lucky, you boys.

MARQUIS

(*To* SULTAN)

We've been very lucky, us boys.

SULTAN

I'm going to break down the door.

MARQUIS

No, no, cousin. We cannot go into her room unless she invites us.

SULTAN

We pay for this house, you and I, and we've been in that room before.

OLD LADY

That's different. She's not getting undressed. She's getting dressed.

(*She sweeps into the boudoir.*)

SULTAN

I say we do these things better in the East. The girl would have been ready on time, or she'd have been dead.

MARQUIS

Oh, charming women make their own rules. And you know that you have found her charming.

SULTAN

Charming! In one generation you have learned to talk like these people. Such words. Charming. She's a woman. You and

I are cousins and so it is sensible to split the expense. We are partners in this woman as we are partners in business. Has nothing to do with charm. So please remember to observe the proper hours and days. And do not fall in love, as you usually do with these women.

MARQUIS

Oh, no, not in love. After all, she's as much yours as mine. (*To guests*) Madame will be with us very soon. In the meantime, supper is in the yellow room.

SULTAN

Cost a fortune.

MARQUIS

Giant truffles, grilled breast of lake peacock.

SULTAN

Cost a fortune.

MARQUIS

Boiled caviar—

SULTAN

And stewed bank notes from the family business.
(*Guests and* MARQUIS *and* SULTAN *exit.*)
(*The lights dim in the ballroom, come up in the boudoir.*)

OLD LADY

(*To a girl, who is crying*)
Now what's the matter?

GIRL

I'm crying.

OLD LADY

You cry the way other people eat . . . right on time.

GIRL

But I am so ashamed of my present life.

OLD LADY

Ach! You never had it so good.

GIRL

I've told you over and over again that I am Cunegonde, Baroness Thunder Ten Tronch of Westphalia.

OLD LADY

Then how come I found you in a Paris gutter?

CUNEGONDE (GIRL)

Last night I dreamed of home. I remembered my wedding day.

OLD LADY

You *married*? You didn't tell me that when I introduced you to these two nice gentlemen.

CUNEGONDE

No, I'm not married. The war came on the day of the wedding.

50

OLD LADY

Is that so? Ah, well, that's the way it happened to most of us. Sometimes war. Sometimes the man changed his mind. Where's the bridegroom?

CUNEGONDE

Dead. Trying to save me from rape . . .

OLD LADY

Died to save you from rape? Oh, aren't men silly?
(OLD LADY *exits from boudoir.*)

CUNEGONDE

Here I am in Paris. I don't even know how I got here. My heart broken. And yet I am forced to glitter, forced to be gay.

(CUNEGONDE *sings*)
Glitter and be gay,
That's the part I play.
Here am I in Paris, France,
Forced to bend my soul
To a sordid role,
Victimized by bitter, bitter circumstance.

Alas for me, had I remained
Beside my lady mother,
My virtue had remained unstained
Until my maiden hand was gained
By some Grand Duke or other.

Ah, 'twas not to be;
Harsh necessity

Brought me to this gilded cage.
Born to higher things,
Here I droop my wings,
Singing of a sorrow nothing can assuage.

(*Suddenly brighter*)
And yet, of course, I rather like to revel, ha, ha!
I have no strong objection to champagne, ha, ha!
My wardrobe is expensive as the devil, ha, ha!
Perhaps it is ignoble to complain ...

Enough, enough
Of being basely tearful!
I'll show my noble stuff
By being bright and cheerful!

Ha, ha ha ha ...

(*Reciting, to music*)
Pearls and ruby rings. . . .
Ah, how can worldly things
Take the place of honor lost?
Can they compensate
For my fallen state,
Purchased as they were at such an awful cost?

Bracelets ... lavalieres ...
Can they dry my tears?
Can they blind my eyes to shame?
Can the brightest brooch
Shield me from reproach?
Can the purest diamond purify my name?

*(Suddenly bright again; singing as she puts on enormous
bracelets)*

And yet, of course, these trinkets are endearing, ha ha!
I'm oh, so glad my sapphire is a star, ha ha!
I rather like a twenty-carat earring, ha ha!
If I'm not pure, at least my jewels are!

(Puts on three more bracelets)

Enough, enough!
I'll *take* their diamond necklace
And show my noble stuff
By being gay and reckless!

Ha ha ha ha ha ...

Observe how bravely I conceal
The dreadful, dreadful shame I feel.
Ha ha ha ha ha, ha ...

(Puts on a giant diamond necklace)

Ha!

(When CUNEGONDE *finishes she is so covered with jewels,
she can hardly be seen. The* OLD LADY *enters at the end of
the aria and immediately begins to rip off the jewels.)*

CUNEGONDE

No! No! I'm cold.

OLD LADY

Only married women can afford to look like whores.

(The boudoir screens disappear as CUNEGONDE *enters the
ballroom. The guests have returned to the waltz. The*
MARQUIS *and the* SULTAN *come running forward. But the*

SULTAN *is faster and rougher, and the gentle* MARQUIS *is left behind. The* SULTAN *takes* CUNEGONDE *into the waltz. When they have waltzed for a minute,* CUNEGONDE *sees* CANDIDE *in the garden. She screams.*)

MARQUIS

What—what is happening my darling—

SULTAN

What's the matter now?

OLD LADY

(*As* CUNEGONDE *is about to faint*)
Madame must be alone. Pray excuse her. She isn't well.

MARQUIS

She isn't well. Oh, cousin, she's so pure, so delicate.

SULTAN

(*Angry*)
So pure, so delicate.

MARQUIS

But, cousin, she's ill, we must send the guests away.
(*The guests begin to say good night, and are followed outside by the hosts. In the boudoir,* CUNEGONDE *is pacing about. The* OLD LADY *beckons to* CANDIDE. CANDIDE, *bewildered, tries to run away.*)

OLD LADY

Come in, come in—You poor boy. Don't be afraid.

CANDIDE

Oh—I couldn't come in here. I'm only looking for work. I'm hungry.

OLD LADY

I've been hungry many times, in many places in the world. I was most highly born and reduced very early—

CANDIDE

Who are you? Whose house is this?
> (CUNEGONDE *appears in the ballroom and* CANDIDE *stands paralyzed in disbelief.*)

> (CANDIDE, *singing*)

Oh. Oh. Is it true?

> (CUNEGONDE, *singing*)

Is it you?

> (CANDIDE)

Cunegonde! Cunegonde! Cunegonde!

> (CUNEGONDE)

Candide! Candide! Can—

OLD LADY

> (*Speaks, interrupting song*)

Your cries of love are natural, but too loud. Remember your benefactors are in the garden.

> (CANDIDE *sings*)

Oh. Oh. Is it true?

55

(CUNEGONDE *sings*)

Is it you?

(CANDIDE)

Cunegonde! Cunegonde! Cunegonde!

(CUNEGONDE)

Candide! Candide! Can—

(CANDIDE)

Oh. Oh. Is it true?

(CUNEGONDE)

Is it you?

(CANDIDE)

Cunegonde!

(CUNEGONDE)

Candide!

(BOTH)

Oh—my—dear—love!

(CANDIDE)

Dearest, how can this be so?
You were dead, you know.
You were shot and bayoneted, too.

(CUNEGONDE)

That is very true.
Ah, but love will find a way.

(CANDIDE)

Then what *did* you do?

(CUNEGONDE)

We'll go into that another day.
Now let's talk of you.
You are looking very well.
Weren't you clever, dear, to survive?

(CANDIDE)

I've a sorry tale to tell.
I escaped more dead than alive.

(CUNEGONDE)

Love of mine, where did you go?

(CANDIDE)

Oh, I wandered to and fro ...

(CUNEGONDE)

Oh, what torture, oh, what pain ...

(CANDIDE)

Holland, Portugal, and Spain ...

(CUNEGONDE)

Ah, what torture ...

(CANDIDE)

Holland, Portu ...

(CUNEGONDE)

Ah, what torture ...

(CANDIDE)

I would do it all again
To find you at last!

(BOTH)

Reunited after so much pain;
But the pain is past.
We are one again,
We are one at last!

One again, one at last
One again, one at last
One, one, one, one,
One
At last!

> (*The* SULTAN *and the* MARQUIS *return to the ballroom.*)

SULTAN

In the name of Allah, who is this man?

CANDIDE

Cunegonde, who is this scoundrel?

MARQUIS

> (*Running to* CUNEGONDE, *who is crying*)

My darling girl, what has happened?

CANDIDE

Gentlemen, I do not understand your presence in this house—
(*Turns, bewildered, to* CUNEGONDE) And come to think of it,
what are you doing here, Cunegonde? Who are these men?
Gentlemen, this lady is my fiancée. I must demand that you
leave her house, this house, whatever house, immediately—

MARQUIS

(*Outraged, draws his sword*)

Your fiancée! You miserable beggar. How dare you—
(*As he advances on* CANDIDE, *the* OLD LADY *appears with a sword and hands it to* CANDIDE. CANDIDE, *anxious not to fight, backs away.*)

CANDIDE

Gentlemen, I have no desire to go about the world dueling. I ask only that you leave peacefully—(*He defends himself from the sword of the* MARQUIS) I do not understand how Cunegonde came to be here, but let me take her away in peace. She will tell you that we have loved since we were the smallest of children—

MARQUIS

(*In love's pain, turns to the* SULTAN)

I can't believe she started so young. It's disgusting.
(*The* OLD LADY *pushes* CANDIDE *into the* MARQUIS. *The* MARQUIS *falls.*)

SULTAN

I will avenge you, my cousin. Our family, despite occasional bickerings and law suits, are as one. (*To* CANDIDE *as they duel*) Do you know that you have killed the President of the Western division of the Far Eastern section of the banking house of—
(*The* OLD LADY *trips the* SULTAN. *He falls onto* CANDIDE's *sword, and drops to the floor.*)

CANDIDE

(*Stands horrified. He throws down his sword and moves toward* CUNEGONDE)

I have killed two men. I don't know why or how. I have killed because of you, and yet I don't even understand why you are here. Answer me, Cunegonde.

OLD LADY

There is no time for all that. These men are of great importance. I have seen enough trouble in my miserable life to tell you that we will all be arrested and executed for this. We must move with speed.

(*She picks up furs and jewel box.*)

CANDIDE

No. I must pay the penalty for what I have done. But before I do, I want you to tell me—

CUNEGONDE

(*Crying out*)

Nothing. Nothing. I am here by accident. The house was empty, and I was starving, and they gave me a little food. (*The* OLD LADY *throws her the jewel box. She catches it*) That is all. They treated me with the greatest respect—How dare you think anything else?

CANDIDE

What are those?

CUNEGONDE

(*Very nervous*)

Jewels. My mother, the Baroness, gave them to me. You have seen her wear them—

CANDIDE

What are you saying Cunegonde? Your mother had a little silver comb, nothing more.

CUNEGONDE

You have insulted me, Candide, and hurt me, too—

OLD LADY

Death stares us in the face, and you are insulted. Be still and allow me to think—
> (*A procession of* PILGRIMS *is seen in the garden. They are moving to march music.*)

PILGRIM FATHER

We are off to the new world. Any and all who wish to slough off the woes of this evil society may join us on our ocean journey to a new life. All who wish to join this loving band, come as sisters and brothers in faith—
> (*The procession moves off.*)

OLD LADY

Come! Come! We will escape by mixing with this pious group.

CUNEGONDE

> (*Stamping her foot*)

But I don't wish to mix with a pious group. I don't wish to go to a new world—
> (*There is the sound of a police whistle.*)

OLD LADY

Police! Be quick—

(*A curtain, on which a ship is painted, is dropped on the Paris scene and the pilgrim procession appears before it. The* OLD LADY, CUNEGONDE *and* CANDIDE *run to join them.*)

Scene 3A

The Scene: A ship painted on a curtain.
At rise: The pilgrim procession is walking toward the gang-
plank.

(PILGRIM FATHER *sings*)
Come, pilgrims, to America!
Come, see the new domains of God!

(ALL *sing*)
Come, pilgrims, to America!
Come, see the new domains of God!

(PILGRIM MOTHER *sings*)
Leave France's wicked sod!
Come and dwell where Satan's hoof has never trod!

(ALL *sing*)
Come, pilgrims, to America!
Where Satan's hoof has never trod!

Alleluia. Alleluia. Alleluia. Alleluia.
Alleluia. Alleluia. Alleluia. Alleluia.

(PILGRIM FATHER *sings*)
We sail to seek God's pardon
Where innocence shall be restored
In that new Eden garden
Where man has not defied his Lord.

(PILGRIM MOTHER *sings*)
Make haste and come aboard!
Come before your hearts in error harden.

(ALL *sing*)
Come, pilgrims, to America!
Where innocence shall be restored!

(CUNEGONDE *and* CANDIDE, *urged on by the* OLD LADY, *sing with the* PILGRIMS)
Alleluia. Alleluia. Alleluia. Alleluia.

(ALL *sing*)
Alleluia. Alleluia. Alleluia. Alleluia.

CAPTAIN
(*Speaks*)
Welcome, travelers. You sail safe on a ship of the greatest comfort. Your staterooms are furnished in imported antique luxury.

PILGRIM FATHER
(*Sharply*)
We wish no luxury. We sail to raise the rocks of America into freedom's hills.

PILGRIMS
Amen.

CAPTAIN
(*To* CUNEGONDE)
You will raise rocks, madame?

CUNEGONDE

Er ...

OLD LADY

(*Quickly*)

Certainly. That's why we have brought our furs.

CAPTAIN

(*To* CANDIDE)

One thousand louis, monsieur, for you, your wife, and her duenna.

CANDIDE

Unfortunately, the lady is not my wife. She will be, however....

CAPTAIN

I'm afraid my ship couldn't accommodate itself to an arrangement of that character.

CANDIDE

No such thought was in my mind. We will occupy two staterooms, I assure you. What arrangement? I don't understand—

CAPTAIN

(*Calling*)

Tickets! Tickets! Two thousand louis.

CUNEGONDE

We have no money. There wasn't time. We had to escape....

OLD LADY

(*Hastily holds out a fur coat*)

This coat of pampampalanium is worth five thousand louis without buttons or lining.

CAPTAIN

I will accept it. You will have no need of it in Mississippi.

PILGRIM FATHER

Mississippi? We were told you sail for the English colony of the north....

CAPTAIN

Yes, yes, of course. We stop at Mississippi for those who wish to disembark there. That seldom happens, so we sail quickly on. (*As a few of the* PILGRIMS *seem to hesitate*) All aboard, ladies and gentlemen. My ship has the best of food, the wittiest of company.

A PILGRIM

Wittiest of company?

PILGRIM FATHER

We spend our time in prayer.

CAPTAIN

Excellent. I know many a witty prayer. All aboard! All aboard for the new world. May you get what you deserve.

(*They move offstage as the curtain rises on Buenos Aires.*)

SCENE 4

The Scene: Buenos Aires. The wharf in front of the Governor's palace; the Governor's palace, terrace and balcony.
At rise: The PILGRIMS, *in chains, are being herded off the ship. They are singing miserable "Alleluias."* MARTIN, *a beggar street cleaner, is moving about.*

CAPTAIN

(*Striding off ship*)
Hello, Martin. You look bad.

MARTIN

I hope so. And I'm sorry to see you looking very well. An evil occupation makes good circulation; evil connections make good complexions. (*He stares at* PILGRIMS) No black slaves this time?

CAPTAIN

Times are hard. I take what I can get. I won't get much for this lot. White slaves are impractical—they show the dirt.

PILGRIM FATHER

(*He is a wreck, but he is still the leader*)
We demand the removal of these chains. Bring us to the representative of France in this land of Canada....
(*The* CAPTAIN *laughs, strides off.*)

MARTIN

(*To* PILGRIMS)

You're not the first he has brought this far afield. This miserable dump is called Buenos Aires. That's the Governor's palace. The Captain is about to put you up on the auction block. (*There is a stunned silence. Then the* PILGRIM FATHER *collapses. The others begin to moan and cry and pray*) Oh, don't carry on so loud. All men are in slavery in this worst of all possible worlds. We choose it for ourselves.

CANDIDE

(*Stumbling to his feet*)

Who are you?

MARTIN

A foreigner. A scholar. A beggar. A street cleaner. A pessimist.

CANDIDE

(*Puzzled*)

Once I knew a man—he looked very like you, sir. He was a great man, kind and wise. He was an optimist and yet he used almost the same words that you . . .

MARTIN

If he was an optimist, he was neither kind nor wise . . . as you must know from the chains around your wrists.

CUNEGONDE

Chains. Chains. I who was born in a castle, daughter to a baron. We had seven German meals a day. I'm hungry. My mother had a sponge bath whenever she called for it, with three maids to do the soaping and one for odds and ends. My brother was white and blond. . . .

OLD LADY

I don't believe a word you say. I never have. Your German castle would not have served as stables for my father's falcons. Ask me who I am. Ask me. (*Nobody asks her*) I am the daughter of the Princess of Palestrina and a man so highly placed, of such piety, that even now I cannot disclose his name. I was beautiful, very spiritual, yet in my sixteenth year, from Constantinople to Odessa, round and round the Crimea, up and down the Black Sea . . . (*Screams*) Ask me what happened to that lovely little princess . . .

CUNEGONDE
(*Very angry*)

A princess! (*To others*) She's my servant. I picked her out of a Paris gutter. . . .

OLD LADY
(*Very, very angry*)

Where you were lying next to me until two rich men came along and took you to their house.

CANDIDE
(*Softly*)

Cunegonde, every hour of this long voyage I have asked you to tell me how it was that I found you in Paris dressed in jewels, living in that great house. I know you are a virtuous woman, but please explain to me. . . .

69

OLD LADY

Oh, what a foolish man you are. Here we are about to be sold into slavery and you think of nothing but her virtue. Virtue. (*She laughs loudly*) Well, that was my last laugh.

CUNEGONDE

(*Shrieking*)
You crone. You filth. You misery.
(CUNEGONDE *and* OLD LADY *fight.*)

MARTIN

I've seen so much evil in my life that simply to keep my balance I am sometimes forced to believe there must be some good in this world. (*Bows to the ladies*) I am grateful to you for reminding me there isn't.
(*The* CAPTAIN *enters.*)

CAPTAIN

Rise up, my slaves, and march to the auction block. Welcome to the land of opportunity.
(MARTIN *moves behind the* CAPTAIN *and cuts the large key chain hanging from the* CAPTAIN's *arm. He throws the keys to the* PILGRIMS. *They unlock their chains as the* CAPTAIN, *unaware of the loss of the keys, exits.*)

PILGRIMS

Thank you! Thank you!

MARTIN

It is typical of the insanity of man that in a minute of danger he stops to say thank you to one who hates him.

PILGRIM FATHER

Thank you! Thank you!
(PILGRIMS *run off*.)

(*Four* OFFICERS *come on stage.* CANDIDE *and* CUNEGONDE *hide.* MARTIN *exits. One of the* OFFICERS *is* MAXIMILLIAN.)

FIRST OFFICER
(*To* MAXIMILLIAN)
And how is His Excellency this morning?

MAXIMILLIAN

He's in a bad humor. He's bored. He's writing a book on the ugliness of C flat. Last week he was writing a book on the beauty of C flat.

SECOND OFFICER

What's C flat?

MAXIMILLIAN

Oh, dear boy, you Spaniards in exile are so uncultured. In Westphalia, I had a tutor from the day I was born. . . .
(*A handsome, middle-aged man appears on the balcony. He is the* GOVERNOR *of Buenos Aires.*)

GOVERNOR

Good morning, gentlemen. I had a wakeful night. I have analyzed every note in the scale and found them wanting. B

double flat used to give me a little pleasure but even that went
last night. . . .

> (CUNEGONDE *sees* MAXIMILLIAN *and screams.* MAXIMILLIAN
> *sees her and screams. They walk toward each other in
> disbelief.*)

CUNEGONDE

I am Cunegonde. I had a brother. He was killed in Westphalia. His name wax Maximillian.

MAXIMILLIAN

(*Pulls her to him*)
My sister. My dear, dead sister. Weren't you dead?

CUNEGONDE

Yes, I was. It's a long story.

MAXIMILLIAN

(*Moves away from her*)
You have fleas, Cunegonde.

GOVERNOR

That . . . that thing is your sister? Dear boy, why did you
bore me with those fantasies of your noble birth?

MAXIMILLIAN

Your Excellency! My sister and I are descended from King
Seidesberger and Queen Desolate of Westphalia. . . .

GOVERNOR

Oh, don't start all that again.

72

MAXIMILLIAN

Now you have really hurt my feelings. Please call your servants to attend my lady sister. Have the largest rooms prepared to suit her station....

GOVERNOR

(*Laughing*)

Most certainly. Bring this ... Bring her in. (OFFICER *leads* CUNEGONDE *to the palace. The* GOVERNOR, *about to exit from balcony, calls down*) Have your sister bathed. Three or four times. Then have her peeled and painted.

CUNEGONDE

(*Speaks softly to* MAXIMILLIAN, *pointing to* CANDIDE)

Dear brother, look who's there.

MAXIMILLIAN

Candide!

CANDIDE

Maximillian!

(CANDIDE, *smiling happily, comes forward;* MAXIMILLIAN, *with cries of surprise, moves to meet him. The* OFFICERS *exit across stage with* CUNEGONDE *and the* OLD LADY.)

MAXIMILLIAN

A miracle, dear brother.

CANDIDE

A miracle, dear brother.

(*They cry.* MARTIN *re-enters and continues his sweeping.*)

73

MAXIMILLIAN

But my sister was dead. And you were dead. And Pangloss was dead....

CANDIDE

No, no. Not in Westphalia. He died again in Lisbon.

MAXIMILLIAN

Oh....

CANDIDE

Ah, there is so much we must tell each other. I will go backwards in the telling. Cunegonde ...

MAXIMILLIAN

I was taken to the burial ground after the Hessian victory. But a good farm woman saw that my eyelids fluttered and she conceived the most tender feelings for me.

CANDIDE

I see that you cannot wait for the story of your sister—

MAXIMILLIAN

Later, a Spanish duchess conceived the most tender feelings for me. I traveled under her protection. Protection! A fine story I could tell you....

CANDIDE

Cunegonde's memory is now confused, I believe, with the horrors she has seen. I don't know what to think of the stories she tells me—

MAXIMILLIAN

. . . And here I was, suddenly in Buenos Aires. (*Delighted*)
My poor Candide. But I shall make your fortune. And my sister
will live in the palace—

CANDIDE

We will be married on the morrow.

MAXIMILLIAN

(*Amazed*)

I don't want to marry you.

CANDIDE

Your sister and I will be married on the morrow.

MAXIMILLIAN

(*Furious*)

You insolent wretch. You still have the impudence to wish
to marry a noble lady? You, of unknown birth, now a broken
beggar . . .

CANDIDE

Maximillian! (*Gently*) That's not a very kind thing to say.
Dr. Pangloss said that all men are created equal. I love your
sister and she loves me. The marriage will take place immediately.

MAXIMILLIAN

You low-born climber. (*Advances on* CANDIDE *in order to
strike him with a glove*) I will send you to the slave block. I will
throw you to the jungle.

75

(CANDIDE *takes the glove from* MAXIMILLIAN *and attempts to slap him. But before he is slapped,* MAXIMILLIAN *drops quietly.* CANDIDE *stands appalled, staring at the body.*)

CANDIDE

(*Moaning*)

Oh, Maximillian, Maximillian. What have I done?

(*The* OLD LADY *saunters out of the palace. She is now done up in fantastic feathers and jewels, and looks worse. She is fanning herself in a great-lady manner. She stands staring at* CANDIDE *as he bends over* MAXIMILLIAN.)

OLD LADY

He looked like the fainting kind.

CANDIDE

I have killed him.

OLD LADY

(*Crossing to* MAXIMILLIAN's *body*)

Killed him? ... He was our protector. The situation here was obvious, although nothing is ever obvious to you....

CANDIDE

What kind of man have I become? I have killed three times. Each time for love. What has love done to me?

OLD LADY

(*To* CANDIDE *as she hears the* GOVERNOR *approaching*)

Hide. Hide. They will arrrest you.

(*She looks around for a hiding place.* MARTIN *motions to a safe place in back of the palace. She grabs* CANDIDE, *pulls him into hiding. After a second, the* GOVERNOR *appears. The* GOVERNOR *crosses to* MAXIMILLIAN's *body.*)

GOVERNOR

(*To* MARTIN)
Street cleaner! Tidy up here, please.
(MARTIN *comes to* MAXIMILLIAN, *covers him with canvas, and begins to drag his body offstage. Three* OFFICERS *appear.*)

FIRST OFFICER

Your Excellency, the young lady is now ready to meet you.

SECOND OFFICER

She says her name is the Baroness Cunegonde.

THIRD OFFICER

She claims that her family . . .

CUNEGONDE

(*Enters in a handsome dress*)
I am not accustomed to appearing alone. Where is my duenna? . . . I've never in my life been alone with men—(*She sees the* GOVERNOR, *and bows*) Oh. Your Excellency.

GOVERNOR

Baroness Cunegonde, you look charming.

CUNEGONDE

Where is my brother?

MARTIN

Excuse me, madame. I have a message for you. Your brother has been called away. But you will meet again (*Softly*) . . . in the end.

(*He drags* MAXIMILLIAN's *body offstage, as* OLD LADY *appears.*)

CUNEGONDE

Oh. How nice. Thank you. Then I will move my baggage to his palace and wait his return. (*Remembering*) But I have no baggage.

GOVERNOR

And your brother has no palace. But I offer you my house.

CUNEGONDE

Thank you, sir. My duenna is with me, and my fiancé.

GOVERNOR

That is rather a large number of people. Perhaps we could put your duenna and your fiancé in a hotel.

CUNEGONDE

I don't understand, sir.

GOVERNOR

Ah, well. How long will it take you to understand?

CUNEGONDE

I don't understand, sir.

GOVERNOR

It's really not very hard if you keep your mind on it. I am offering you a wing of my house and a wing of my heart.

CUNEGONDE

I don't understand, sir.

GOVERNOR
(Sighs)
Perhaps it will all take too long.
(He starts back into palace.)

OLD LADY
(Desperate)
I think I understand. You are offering this innocent girl a wing of your heart....

GOVERNOR

Yes. Because my heart has wings and flies about. I think it best to tell you that now.

CUNEGONDE

I don't understand, sir....

GOVERNOR

I'll try once more.

(He sings)
Poets have said
Love is undying, my love;

79

Don't be misled;
They were all lying, my love.

Love's on the wing,
But now while he hovers,
Let us be lovers.
One soon recovers, my love.

Soon the fever's fled,
For love's a transient blessing.
Just a week in bed,
And we'll be convalescing.

Why talk of morals
When springtime is flying?
Why end in quarrels,
Reproaches and sighing,

> Crying
> For love?

For love undying, my love,
Is not worth trying, my love.
Never, my love,
Mention forever, my love.

Let it be lively,
Let it be lovely,
And light as a song,
But don't let it last too long!

OLD LADY

(*Speaking very quickly*)
His Excellency is asking for your hand—

CUNEGONDE

(*Deeply hurt*)

Hand? Oh, oh, sire—you must not take advantage of my innocence....

OLD LADY

The great gentleman is proposing marriage.

GOVERNOR

(*Laughs*)

I should like you to be my wife.

(OLD LADY *waves to* CUNEGONDE, *nodding her head with violence.*)

CUNEGONDE

(*Softly*)

Leave me, sire. I must have time to think it over.

(*The* GOVERNOR *bows, and exits.*)

OLD LADY

(*To* CUNEGONDE)

We are starving and have just been removed from chains. The greatest lord in South America wishes to marry you, and yet you ...

CUNEGONDE

But I love Candide. I can't marry another man.

OLD LADY

Candide will be hunted down and executed for the murder ... (*When* CUNEGONDE *looks bewildered and frightened*) ... of the Marquis and the Sultan. The Paris police are on their way

81

here now. It is your duty to marry the Governor and save Candide.

CUNEGONDE

But I don't love this man and I don't want to be unfaithful....

OLD LADY

Look. Think of it this way. Marrying another man is no more unfaithful than sleeping with another man.

CUNEGONDE

Oooooh! Is that true? You are so worldly.

OLD LADY

You have to live. You have to get along as best you can.

(OLD LADY *sings and begins dancing to the music of a tango*)

I was not born in Buenos Aires.
My father came from Rovno Gubernya.
But now I'm here ... I'm dancing a tango:
                Di dee di!
                Dee di dee di!
I am easily assimilated.
I am so easily assimilated.

I never learned a human language.
My father spoke a High Middle Polish.
In one half-hour I'm talking in Spanish:
                Por favor!
                Toreador!
I am easily assimilated.
I am so easily assimilated.

It's easy, it's ever so easy!
I'm Spanish, I'm suddenly Spanish!

And you must be Spanish, too.
Do like the natives do.
These days you have to be
In the majority.

    (*Two local* SEÑORES *enter, and serenade the* OLD LADY)
Tus labios rubí
Dos rosas que se abren a mí,
Conquistan mi corazón,
Y sólo con
Una canción.

    (OLD LADY *sings, imitating them*)
Tus labios rubí
Drei-viertel Takt, mon très cher ami,
Oui oui, sí sí, ja ja ja, yes, yes, da, da.
Je ne sais quoi.

    (SEÑORES *sing as a crowd begins to gather*)
Me muero, me sale una hernia!

    (OLD LADY *sings*)
A long way from Rovno Gubernya!

    (ALL, *including* CUNEGONDE, *who has caught the spirit*)
Tus labios rubí
Dos rosas que se abren a mí
Conquistan mi corazón
Y sólo con
Una divina canción ...

De tus labios rubí
Rubí! Rubí!

(*Everybody is dancing. At the end of the dance* CUNE-
GONDE *is cheerful.*)

CUNEGONDE
(*Speaking*)

Do you know what?

OLD LADY

What?

CUNEGONDE

I've made up my mind. I will marry the Governor. I will save
Candide. My heart breaks.

(CUNEGONDE *runs into the palace. The crowd exits. The*
OLD LADY *smiles and nods.* MARTIN *reappears.* CANDIDE
returns from his hiding place.)

OLD LADY
(*To* CANDIDE)

You must leave. They will arrest you.

CANDIDE

I can't leave Cunegonde.

OLD LADY

Go make your fortune and come back for us. Cunegonde will
be safe. The Governor suggested that she stay and read to him
at night. I think he's blind. Go quickly.

CANDIDE

That's very kind of him, but ...

OLD LADY

Go quick. Quick. Go.
(*She exits.*)

CANDIDE

Where shall I go?

MARTIN

What difference does it make where anybody goes? Be on your way, boy.

CANDIDE

There is no place for me. Wherever I go I am beaten and starved. I mean no harm to anybody and yet I have murdered three men in the name of love. I am alone now....

MARTIN

So are we all. It is the worst of all possible worlds, and if it wasn't, we would make it so.

CANDIDE

No, no. Although I have seen a great deal of evil, it is my conviction that man is ... (*He chokes on the words*) honest and kind and ... well ... and ... well, there must be a place where he *is* honest and kind and good and noble and ...

MARTIN

There is such a place. And if I thought you believed that foolishness I would send you there. They would like you.

CANDIDE

I do believe that foolishness. I mean, I do believe what I believe, but I don't believe there's such a place in this world. I mean there is such a place, of course, but I haven't found it—(*Almost in tears*) Oh, I am tired. And I don't understand anything any more.

MARTIN

In the highest peak of the Andes there is a country called Eldorado. I was born there. For hundreds of years . . . (*Points to palace*) their armies have been trying to find it. They break their backs on the mountains, and the people of Eldorado come out to stare at the soldiers. They do not understand what a soldier is, nor do they care that he came to kill them. They give him a house, send him to school, give him useful work, and make him smile. No enemy soldier has ever wanted to come back.

CANDIDE

Paradise.

MARTIN

No, no. Not Paradise. They would think Paradise a dream for children.

CANDIDE

Why did you leave such a place?

MARTIN

They put me out. They said I was the first man ever born there who wasn't happy. They said I was diseased and could not stay with them. They asked me to go. Perhaps they were right. I don't believe that man is honest, or kind, or good.

CANDIDE

Oh, I do, sir. I do believe it. I haven't anything more. Would they take me in?

MARTIN

Yes. They will take any man who comes in peace. (*Throws him a compass*) Go up the Andes and turn left. Here is an emerald compass that points straight to a diamond hill. There's an elephant at the door. He will carry you in. Give him my regards.

(*The* GOVERNOR, CUNEGONDE *and the* OLD LADY *appear on the balcony.*)

(CANDIDE *sings*)

Once again I must be gone,
Moving on to Eldorado.
Shall my hopes be answered there?
Is that land so good and fair?
Though that Eden well may be,
Though it shine however brightly,
Still no bright yonder can delight me;
Cunegonde won't be there to share it with me.

(CUNEGONDE *sings*)

Though it may seem
I am discarding Candide,
Truly my scheme
Is for safeguarding Candide.
Though I abhor
This loveless connection,
I'll feign affection
For your protection, Candide.

(GOVERNOR *sings*)

Why should I wed?
Marriage is awful, you know.

87

Passion is dead
Once it is lawful, you know.
No, I'll not wed.
That would be the worst thing.
After the first fling
Women are awful, you know.

(OLD LADY *sings*)

Haven't I got brains?
I'm devilishly witty!
We were just in chains, and now we're sitting pretty!

(CUNEGONDE)	(OLD LADY)	
Farewell my love	If you've got brains and	
Ah farewell my love	you're clever and	
Aaaaaaaaah!	witty	
	You can make out and	
	wind up sitting	
	pretty!	
	Aaaaaaaaaaaaaah!	*Simul-*
		taneously
(GOVERNOR)	(CANDIDE)	
No, for passion is dead	Farewell my love fare-	
when it's lawful you	well!	
know.	Farewell Cunegonde	
No, no, no, marriage is	farewell farewell!	
awful you know.	Aaaaaaaaaaaaaah!	
Aaaaaaaaaah!		

MARTIN

(*Speaks*)

Well, they all believe what they are screaming. We'll see.

(CUNEGONDE)

Though it may seem I
    am discarding Can-
    dide
Truly my scheme is for
    safeguarding Candide
Though I abhor this
    loveless connection
Farewell to my love
Farewell to my love
Farewell to my love
Farewell to my love

(OLD LADY)

Haven't I got brains
I'm devilishly witty
We were just in chains
And now we're sitting
    pretty
Sitting pretty
You've got to have
    brains
You've got to have
    brains
You've got to have
    brains to live.

Simul-
taneously

(GOVERNOR)

Why should I wed
Marriage is awful you
    know
Passion is dead once it is
    lawful you know
Women are awful after
    the first fling
No, no, I'll not wed
No, no, I'll not wed
No, no, I'll not wed, no.

(CANDIDE)

Though that Eden may
    well be
Though it shine how-
    ever brightly
What bright yonder can
    delight me
Farewell to my love
Farewell to my love
Farewell to my love.

(*At the end of the quartet,* CANDIDE *lifts the compass, raises it, smiles, and runs off.*)

Curtain

89

ACT TWO

ACT TWO

The Scene: Same as Buenos Aires, Act One. But now we see a room of the palace. SAILORS *are loading a boat. There is a group of miserable-looking* PEONS *sitting onstage.*

At rise: The OLD LADY *is sitting on the steps. Off the balcony, in the room, the* GOVERNOR *and* CUNEGONDE *are playing chess. The* GOVERNOR *is waiting for* CUNEGONDE *to move her chess piece. The room is filled with fine pictures and fine books.*

CUNEGONDE
(*At chess table, speaking*)

Hot, isn't it?

GOVERNOR

No.

CUNEGONDE

It was cold yesterday, wasn't it?

GOVERNOR

No.

CUNEGONDE

It will rain tonight, won't it?

GOVERNOR

Wherever you are, it's raining all the time.

93

OLD LADY

Hoihh!

SAILOR

What's the matter, lady?

OLD LADY

I'm homesick for everywhere but here.

(She sings)
No doubt you'll think I'm giving in
                    To petulance and malice,
But in candor I am forced to say
That I'm sick of gracious living in
                    This stuffy little palace.
And I wish that I could leave today.
I have suffered a lot
And I'm certainly not
  Unaware that this life has its black side.
I have starved in a ditch,
I've been burned for a witch,
  And I'm missing the half of my backside.
I've been beaten and whipped
And repeatedly stripped,
  I've been forced into all kinds of whoredom;
But I'm finding of late
That the very worst fate
  Is to perish of comfort and BOREDOM.

GOVERNOR

(Speaking)
Quiet.

(CUNEGONDE *sings to* GOVERNOR)

It was three years ago
As you very well know
 That you said we would soon have a wedding;
Every day you forget
What you promised, and yet
 You continue to rumple my bedding.
I'll no longer bring shame
On my family name.
 I had rather lie down and be buried;
No, I'll not lead the life
Of an unwedded wife.
 Tell me, when are we going to be MARRIED?

GOVERNOR

(*Speaking*)

Quiet.

(OLD LADY *sings*)

I was once, what is more,
Nearly sawed in four
 By a specially clumsy magician;
And you'd think I would feel
After such an ordeal
 That there's charm in my present position.
But I'd far rather be
In a tempest at sea,
 Or a bloody North African riot,
Than to sit in this dump

On what's left of my rump
>And put up with this terrible QUIET.

>(CUNEGONDE, *joining in*)
When are we going to be MARRIED?

>(OLD LADY *sings*)
Comfort and boredom and QUIET....   *Simul-*
taneously
>(CUNEGONDE *sings, crescendo*)
When are we going to be—

>(GOVERNOR *sings*)
QUIET!

CUNEGONDE
>(*Speaking to the* GOVERNOR)
I had a dream.

GOVERNOR
Great mistake to talk about your dreams.

CUNEGONDE
And in my dream, my dear mother, the Baroness, came to me.
She is now a princess. And you know what she told me?
She told me that you must marry me.

GOVERNOR
(*Rings a bell. In a minute, two* OFFICERS *will appear in answer
to the bell*)
Tell your mother to go back where she came from and take
you with her.

96

CUNEGONDE

My mother said that if you do not marry me this week, I must leave you.

OLD LADY

I have told you over and over again that such talk does not lead to marriage. Why don't you learn to cook?

CUNEGONDE

(*Softly to* OLD LADY)
He adores me. He will never allow me to leave. (*To* GOVERNOR) And so I will pack the few miserable clothes that you have bought me, and take passage on the next boat.

GOVERNOR

(*Who has been whispering to the* OFFICERS)
No need to wait for the next boat, sweetheart. The cotton boat goes immediately.

(*The* OFFICERS, *with great speed, put heavy sacks over* CUNEGONDE *and the* OLD LADY *and bundle them off.*)

(*A* PEON *rises suddenly and begins pointing. The others rise in great excitement.* MARTIN *comes in to join the crowd.* CANDIDE *enters. He is bowed down with gold and jewels.*)

CANDIDE

Good evening, good folk. (*To* MARTIN) My dear good friend. How glad I am to see you.

A WOMAN

(*In crowd*)

Look at that. A rich man kisses a beggar.

A PEON

(*Frightened*)

Where does such a man come from?

ANOTHER WOMAN

Look at the jewels on him. Maybe he ain't human.

A PEON

What's in the bags, stranger?

CANDIDE

Gold. And I'd like to share it with you.

A WOMAN

I told you he wasn't human.

(CANDIDE *smiles, dips into a bag and gives out large gold coins. The crowd draws back as if frightened. Then they pick up the gold with cries of pleasure.*)

A WOMAN

Kind stranger.

A MAN

Blessings from the poor.

A WOMAN

A man of charity.

(*The noise has brought the* GOVERNOR *to the balcony.*)

A WOMAN

This ain't gold. Ain't got no picture of a king. Ain't got no picture of a big-nosed general.

MARTIN

They don't need a king or a big-nosed general in Eldorado. They've never been at war, nor pronounced its name.

A WOMAN

(*To* CANDIDE)

You left such a place? To come back here?

CANDIDE

Yes. I came back to find the woman I love.

A WOMAN

My God. He's crazy.

A MAN

There's no such place where they don't have soldiers and war.

CANDIDE

There is such a place.

(CANDIDE *sings*)

Up a seashell mountain,
Across a primrose sea,
To a jungle fountain
High up in a tree;

Then down a primrose mountain,
Across a seashell sea,

To a land of happy people,
Just and kind and bold and free.

(CHORUS *sings*)
To Eldorado...

(CANDIDE *sings*)
They bathe each dawn in a golden lake,
Emeralds hang upon the vine.
All is there for all to take,
Food and God and books and wine.

They have no words for fear and greed,
For lies and war, revenge and rage.
They sing and dance and think and read.
They live in peace, and die of age.

(CHORUS *sings*)
In Eldorado...

(CANDIDE *sings*)
They gave me home, they called me friend,
They taught me how to live in grace.
Seasons passed without an end
In that sweetly blessed place.

But I grew sad and could not stay;
Without my love my heart was cold.
So they sadly sent me on my way
With gracious gifts of gems and gold.

(CHORUS *sings*)
From Eldorado...

(CANDIDE *sings*)

Good-bye, they said, we pray you
May safely cross the sea.
Go, they said, and may you
Find your bride-to-be.

Then past the jungle fountain,
Along a silver shore,
I've come by sea and mountain
To be with my love once more.

(CHORUS *sings*)

From Eldorado ...

(CANDIDE *sings*)

To be with my love once more.
(*The crowd exits as the two* OFFICERS *cross stage carrying* CUNEGONDE *and the* OLD LADY, *who are covered up completely and wrapped as bundles. There are muffled cries from within the bundles.*)

CANDIDE

What was that? It was a woman's voice.

GOVERNOR

(*Appears on balcony*)

There are no female bales of cotton, sir. Perhaps the sun has tired you.

CANDIDE

(*Bows to* GOVERNOR)

I wish to ask audience of Your Excellency. I have come to find the Baroness Cunegonde.

GOVERNOR

Oh, yes . . . Allow me the honor of joining you.
(*He disappears.*)

CANDIDE

That's funny talk. It's no honor to join me.

MARTIN

That's the way the rich talk to the rich.

CANDIDE

The people of Eldorado made me very rich with gold and jewels. But I won't ever talk like that. I am a simple man—

MARTIN

Yes, you are. But His Excellency is not simple. I advise you to take care.

CANDIDE

Nothing to take care about. As soon as Cunegonde joins us, we will all take ship for home. Life will be good for us now—

MARTIN
(*Softly*)

You will take me with you?

CANDIDE

You are my friend and my benefactor. What I have is yours, now and always.

MARTIN

(*Deeply upset. His voice rising*)

Are you a man who remembers those who helped you? Are you a kind man, are you a just man?—(*Screams in pain*) If you are a good man, I don't want to know you. It's too late, I am too old. I don't want to start thinking all over again—

CANDIDE

I am not a good man. So please don't cry.

GOVERNOR

(*Reappears, with* OFFICER, *who is carrying a wine tray*)

Now, sir, a glass of wine. It's a modest wine because it has nothing to be immodest about.

CANDIDE

Thank you. I have come only to fetch the Baroness Cunegonde—

GOVERNOR

What lovely emeralds. I like emeralds.

(*At a signal, two more* OFFICERS *appear.*)

CANDIDE

Would you bring me to the Baroness Cunegonde?

GOVERNOR

What lovely emeralds. *I like emeralds.*

MARTIN

(*Carefully to* GOVERNOR)

My friend would like to contribute to your favorite charity.

(*To* CANDIDE) You never pay the rich. You endow a favorite charity.
(*He gives a bag of gold to the* GOVERNOR.)

GOVERNOR

Thank you. This gold will go to the Royal Insane Asylum. Now. The Baroness Cunegonde would not consent to stay here. I begged her to remain in my care—although I am a Governor and not a governess, as a rule—but when she found you were gone, she demanded to follow you to Europe.

CANDIDE

(*Deeply upset*)
To Europe! We must find a ship! (*Spanish* LADIES *and* OFFICERS *enter*) We must find a ship! Immediately.

GOVERNOR

The last ship sailed a few minutes ago. But be patient. In a few months—

CANDIDE

No, sir. I can't be patient. I will buy a boat. I will buy ten boats—

FIRST OFFICER

A boat, sir?

GOVERNOR

There is no boat in this harbor, except my pleasure schooner, the *Santa Rosalia*.

FIRST OFFICER

But Your Excellency, the *Santa Rosalia* is a shell. It has not been used for many years . . .

GOVERNOR

Nonsense! The *Santa Rosalia* is *entirely* seaworthy.

FIRST LADY

A fine boat.

SECOND LADY

A famous boat.

CANDIDE

I will buy your boat. Here are ten thousand pieces of gold.

GOVERNOR

Who can refuse a lover? But I am not a merchant, and I do not sell boats.

CANDIDE

Oh, I could not accept so large a gift, sir.

GOVERNOR

I understand your feelings. Put twenty thousand pieces of gold on the steps. Buenos Aires needs *two* insane asylums.
(*Puzzled,* CANDIDE *puts down two bags of gold.*)

SECOND OFFICER

Have a pleasant trip.

THIRD OFFICER

The wind and tide are favorable.

Bon voyage.

GOVERNOR

My regards to the Baroness Cunegonde.
(MARTIN *and* CANDIDE *exit*.)

(GOVERNOR *sings*)

Bon voyage, dear fellow,
Dear benefactor of your fellow-man!
May good luck attend you.
Do come again and see us when you can.

(CHORUS *sings*)

Bon voyage, dear fellow,
Dear benefactor of your fellow-man!
May good luck attend you.
Do come again and see us when you can.

(GOVERNOR *sings*)

Oh, but I'm bad. Oh, but I'm bad,
Playing such a very dirty trick on such a fine lad!
I'm a low cad, I'm a low cad:
Always when I do this sort of thing it makes me so sad,
   Ever so sad!
   Oh, but I'm bad!
   Ever so bad!

(ALL *sing*)

Bon voyage!

(MEN *of* CHORUS *sing*)

Bon voyage, we'll see ya.
Do have a jolly trip across the foam.

(WOMEN *of* CHORUS *sing*)

Santa Rosalia,
Do have a safe and pleasant journey home.

(*Full* CHORUS *sings*)

Bon voyage!

(GOVERNOR *sings*)

I'm so rich that my life is an utter bore:
There is just not a thing that I need.
My desires are as dry as an applecore,
And my only emotion is *greed*.

Which is why, though I've nothing to spend it for,
I have swindled this gold from Candidi-di-di-di-dide,
    Poor Candide!

GOVERNOR

(*Looks out to sea, speaks*)

Oh, dear, the water's up to his neck—well, there goes his
head.

(GOVERNOR *sings*)

But I never would swindle the humble poor,
For you can't get a turnip to bleed.
When you swindle the rich you get so much more,
Which is why I have swindled Candide.
    Oh, dear, I fear

He's going down, he's going to drown!
Ah, poor Candide!

(ALL *sing*)

Bon voyage, best wishes.
Seems to have been a bit of sabotage.
Things don't look propitious,
Still from the heart we wish you bon voyage.
Bon voyage!!!!

(*The song ends as the scene at Buenos Aires blacks out and the
lights come up on a raft in the middle of the ocean.*)

Scene 1A

The Scene: Travels from Buenos Aires to Venice.
At rise: MARTIN *and* CANDIDE *are on the raft.* CANDIDE *is rowing,*
MARTIN *is fishing with a strip of cloth.*

CANDIDE

He gave us a boat that sank and sold us a boat that was nothing but a shell. Did he wish to kill us, and why? He was a rich man and yet he cheated us. What for? He was such a cultured fellow—it cannot be true.

MARTIN
(*Wearily*)
It cannot be true, but it is true.

CANDIDE

I don't understand. When I was poor and people were mean and cruel to me, I told myself that the rags of the poor smell bad, and bad smells make people frightened, and fright makes people angry, and anger makes people—

MARTIN

And you told yourself that if ever you were rich you would smell sweet, and thus your troubles would be at an end. Well, you are still very rich and you will still have trouble because now you cannot be ignored, and no man will rest until he has stripped you. Or he will wait, frightened, for you to strip him.

CANDIDE

But what is the use of money unless it buys happiness?

MARTIN

Even on a log, starving, in the middle of an ocean, you talk like a sun-touched child. I'll make you into a pessimist before this voyage is over. Or nature will.

CANDIDE

I love nature, or I used to.

MARTIN

Then tell your love that we are starving and have not eaten for two days.

CANDIDE

We will survive.

MARTIN

Why do you wish to survive?

CANDIDE

Because I am convinced that there is as much good as there is evil in the world, and I am determined to find the good in others and in myself—

MARTIN

As much good as there is evil. In a world where men march across continents to kill each other without even asking why. Where the scientist strives to prolong life and at the same min-ute invents weapons to wipe it out. Where children are taught the rules of charity and kindness until they grow to the age where they would be considered insane if they put the rules into practice. Where half the world starves and the other half diets— (*A shark's head appears, and* MARTIN *looks at it with interest*) A pretty fish. It has strange eyes.

CANDIDE

Yes, much of what you say is true, and many of my dreams have faded. But I still believe in the essential goodness of the human heart—

MARTIN

The human heart is cowardly and hypocritical, and is not a heart at all: it is more vicious than the monsters of the sea that rise around us now. We would be safer in the arms of a shark than in the arms of a brother—

(*The shark reappears and yanks* MARTIN *from the boat.* MARTIN *quietly disappears into the sea.* CANDIDE, *not knowing that his friend has gone, continues to speak.*)

CANDIDE

You've had a bad life, my friend, but I still have enough Eldorado gold and gems to put charity to the test. Sometimes I wonder if I should ever have left there—Ah, well, we'll never have to grovel or beg, you and I, and we'll give to those who need it and sit ourselves down to live and think in peace. There is much that worries me, I admit to you, and I am not the optimist I once was. But we'll live quietly when we find my Cunegonde, and you'll feel better when you hear the laughter of my babies—(*He discovers* MARTIN *is not there and begins to shout*) Martin! Martin! Where are you?

(PANGLOSS *climbs aboard the raft.*)

CANDIDE

Dr. Pangloss . . . I left you in Lisbon. I thought you were dead.

PANGLOSS

I thought I was dead. But the wife of a doctor, a pretty woman—pretty for a doctor's wife—saved me. She was very much in love with me, sweet girl, and we ran away together. But we were captured by pirates, and I have been a miserable galley slave for many years—(*He starts to cry.* CANDIDE *holds him in his arms*) When you've swallowed a lot of water, you cry very easily. I am so hungry. (*Bright as a scholar*) Salt water is a purgative, my boy—for the body and for the mind.

CANDIDE

You'll be safe now. You'll have all you want to eat, and a carriage to ride in—(*As if to a child*) What would you like most? I am a very rich man.

PANGLOSS

I would like most to hear you repeat the golden rules of a high-minded Westphalian man.

CANDIDE

Honor, the generous heart of all mankind—No, sir, I *can't* say those words any more.

PANGLOSS
(*Softly*)
You break the heart of an old man.

CANDIDE

(*Struggling*)

The heart of mankind is a generous heart. The honor of a man is all he needs on life's journey. The poor must be respected, and so must the rich since they are always with us—

(PANGLOSS *smiles with pleasure. The lights dim as the raft moves off and Venice comes into place.*)

The Scene: Venice. A gambling house.
At rise: People are already at the gaming tables. The tables
are presided over by FERONE, *the owner of the gambling house.*
The guests are masked. From time to time the masks will be
removed. Among the people at the table is SIGNORA SOFRONIA,
who is the OLD LADY. *She is very dressed up.*

CROUPIER

Faites vos jeux, messieurs, dames.
   (*The guests sing the words, "Money, money, money."*
   The wheel turns and all heads turn with it. The wheel
   stops and there are cries from the losers. SIGNORA SOFRONIA
   steps out, her arms loaded with chips.)

FERONE

   (*To all, as he moves forward to* SOFRONIA)
Sixteen. And only one lady bet on the number. Allow me to
congratulate you, Signora Sofronia.

CROUPIER

Faites vos jeux—messieurs, dames.
   (*The guests return to gambling.*)

FERONE

   (*Taking the chips from* SOFRONIA)
I told you *not* to play sixteen. Have a little sense. You can't
win every time. They are already suspicious of you. (*A chip*

drops. SOFRONIA *scrambles on her hands and knees for it.* FERONE *puts his foot on the chip*) Get up. You're not in Rovno Gubernya. (*He hurries to great a new group*) Signor Duca. (*To an elderly lady, who ras entered with four very* TALL GIRLS) Madame La Duchesse. You were not with us last night.

LA DUCHESSE

No, I was with my astrologer. And tonight, with his advice, I shall win back the fortune I've lost to you. (PREFECT OF POLICE *enters and crosses between them. She points to him*) Isn't that the Prefect of Police?

FERONE

Yes, madame.

LA DUCHESSE

Strange. Last week he lost his fortune and vowed to kill himself. I went to the funeral. Very puzzling isn't it? Ah, well. (*Introducing the very* TALL GIRLS) My English cousins.

FOUR TALL GIRLS
(*All together*)

Hudda da.

LA DUCHESSE

They're so shy. Their father owns Africa. They're too young to play. Give them a little sugar water. I will play on number fifteen.

CROUPIER

Faites vos jeux, messieurs, dames.

FERONE

(*To* TALL GIRLS, *as* LA DUCHESSE *moves away*)

Dull for you to stand around.

A TALL GIRL

Nowt tat tall.

FERONE

May I lend you a few chips?

FOUR TALL GIRLS

(*All together*)

How madly divine. What are chips?

FERONE

Chips are money.

FOUR TALL GIRLS

Aww.

FERONE

I wish you great luck.

FOUR TALL GIRLS

(*All together*)

Chips are money. How divinely mad.

(*They hurry to the table.*)

FERONE

(*To* SOFRONIA)

Put your foot under the table and press the pedal to the left.
Left.

(*She moves to the table.*)

CROUPIER

Faites vos jeux—

> (*The wheel turns. This time most of the guests scream
> in delight.* FERONE *leaves the table angrily.* SOFRONIA *joins
> him.*)

SOFRONIA

I did just as you told me. I put my foot on the pedal and
pressed to the *right*. What happened?

FERONE

What happened is that you're a fool.

SOFRONIA

Who, me?

FERONE

I told you to press to the *left*. One more mistake and you'll be
out of here.

> (SOFRONIA *sings*)

I have always been wily and clever
At deceiving and swindling and such,
And I feel just as clever as ever,
But I seem to be losing my touch.
Yes, I'm clever, but where does it get me?
> (*Indicates* FERONE)
My employer gets all of my take;
All I get is my daily spaghetti,
While he gorges on truffles and steak.

What's the use?
What's the use?

There's no profit in cheating,
It's all so defeating
And wrong,
Oh, so wrong!
If you just have to pass it along.

(FERONE *sings*)

That old hag is no use in this gyp-joint;
Not a sou have I made on her yet,
And the one thing that pays in this clip-joint
Is my fraudulent game of roulette.
But I have to pay so much protection
(*Indicates* PREFECT OF POLICE)
To the chief of police and his men
That each day when he makes his collection
I'm a poor man all over again.

(OLD LADY *and* FERONE *sing together*)

What's the use?
What's the use
Of dishonest endeavor
And being so clever?
It's wrong,
Oh, so wrong!
If you just have to pass it along.

(PREFECT OF POLICE *sings*)

It's a very fine thing to be prefect,
Shaking down all the gamblers in town.
My position has only one defect:

That there's somebody shaking *me* down.
(*Indicates a* FAT MAN)
For this fellow unhappily knows me,
And he's on to the game that I play,
And he threatens to shame and expose me
If I do not incessantly pay.

(OLD LADY, FERONE, *and* PREFECT OF POLICE *sing together*)

What's the use?
What's the use
Of this sneaky conniving
And slimy contriving?
It's wrong,
Oh, so wrong,
If you just have to pass it along.

(FAT MAN *sings*)

I could live very well by extortion,
But I simply can't keep what I earn,
For I haven't a sense of proportion,
And roulette is my only concern.
I've a system that's fiendishly clever,
Which I learnt from a croupier friend,
And I *should* go on winning forever—
But I *do* seem to lose in the end.

(OLD LADY, FERONE, PREFECT OF POLICE *and* FAT MAN *sing together*)

What's the use?
What's the use—

(OLD LADY *sings*)

Of this cheating and plotting?
You end up with notting!

(*They continue singing, repeating the refrains. At the
end of the song,* SOFRONIA *moves to bedroom, rings a bell,
and collapses. In a second,* CUNEGONDE *appears, carrying
a foot bath. She is dressed as a scrub woman. She kneels,
and takes off* SOFRONIA'S *shoes.*)

SOFRONIA

When you've been born a princess your feet always hurt.

CUNEGONDE

(*Weary, without interest*)

So you've told me before. Were you really born a princess?

SOFRONIA

(*As she puts her feet in bath*)

What difference does it make?

CUNEGONDE

(*Takes off her shoes, puts her feet into foot bath. Points out to
the gambling room*)

How did you do tonight?

SOFRONIA

Fine. Fine. In a few weeks we'll have a nice little nest egg, and
we'll leave.

CUNEGONDE

Where'll we go?

SOFRONIA

(Cheerful, but without conviction)

What do you mean, where'll we go? We'll buy a refined wardrobe, a carriage with a crest, put a footman on the box—What do you mean, where'll we go? The world is open, waiting for us.

CUNEGONDE

It hasn't acted that way.

SOFRONIA

We'll drive to Rome. I have relatives there, most highly placed. (CUNEGONDE *laughs.* SOFRONIA *bristles, then laughs with her*) Listen, my girl, we're lucky. We slept on mattresses this week.

CUNEGONDE

There was a time when I didn't think that so lucky.

SOFRONIA

Now none of that talk. What do you think most people get in this world—what they want? You do the best you can.

CUNEGONDE

Yes, you've told me that before.

SOFRONIA

Tomorrow will come. And it will be better.

(The lights dim in the bedroom and come up in the ball-room as CANDIDE *and* PANGLOSS *enter the room. They are in fine clothes, and* CANDIDE *carries his gold in jeweled bags. They are given masks by an attendant.* FERONE *comes forward.)*

CROUPIER

Faites vos jeux, messieurs, dames.

PANGLOSS

Our apologies for intruding.

FERONE

Yes, sir?

PANGLOSS

We are searching for a lady, and our private informants tell us that she may be in Venice, and that here, where the highest of society gathers—

FERONE

What is the name of the lady?

CANDIDE

The Baroness Cunegonde.
(FERONE *shakes his head.*)

FERONE

I'm afraid the name means nothing to me.

PANGLOSS

Ah, well. We'll continue on. We've posted large rewards in Brussels, in Paris, in Bordeaux, in Milan, all over Venice—(*To* FERONE, *indicating* CANDIDE) His great fortune brings him no pleasure—

FERONE

His great fortune brings him no pleasure? (*Quickly*) Wait. Perhaps the lady is here. Names do not stay with me. Do be at home. What does the Baroness look like?

PANGLOSS

It has been a long time since my friend has seen her.

CANDIDE

(*Smiles sadly*)
She will not have changed. She is blonde, delicate, charming—

FERONE

Then certainly she is here. She must be here. Ah, ladies—a distinguished stranger—(*He pushes forward the four* TALL GIRLS) The Ladies Mary Cutely, Mary Toothly, Mary Soothly, and Mary Richmond. Is it possible—

(CANDIDE *shakes his head. The* MARQUIS *and the* SULTAN, *of the Paris episode, pass by.* CANDIDE *stares at them, starts to follow them, then turns back, very puzzled.* FERONE *has moved into the bedroom.* PANGLOSS *moves toward the roulette table.*)

CROUPIER

Faites vos jeux—messieurs, dames.

LA DUCHESSE

Ten thousand on number fifteen.

FAT MAN

Twenty thousand on six.

DUKE OF NAPLES

Twenty-five thousand on eleven.

A LADY

Twenty-five thousand on twelve.

PANGLOSS

My! A lifetime in a minute. I bet five lire on number five.

DUKE OF NAPLES

No bets under a thousand are allowed here.

PANGLOSS

Oh, goodness. Oh, my.

CANDIDE

Here's a hundred thousand. Play if it gives you pleasure.

FERONE

(*In bedroom, stares at* SOFRONIA *and* CUNEGONDE, *who are still bathing their feet*)

Is this what I pay you for?

SOFRONIA

You ain't paid us.

FERONE

Now listen. There's a country boy out there, all dressed up and loaded with gold. Give him a sad story about your life. Tell him all about your mother and father—any nonsense. If you can't take him, you'll be out of here tonight. Both of you. Get to work. Be smart.

(*He leaves.*)

SOFRONIA

Smart. He has to tell us to be smart.

CUNEGONDE

Ah. I'm sick of being smart. It ends up being hungry.

SOFRONIA

You stop that talk. Just do your part. We'll be in Rome in the
morning.
(*Lights dim in bedroom, come up again in ballroom.*)

CANDIDE

(*Speaks to* PANGLOSS *and points to the* SULTAN *and the* MARQUIS)
I have seen ghosts or the sons of ghosts. I killed those men in
Paris in a duel.

PANGLOSS

Is that so? (*Holds out chips*) Look. I am winning. But I don't
feel it's proper to chance your money—

CANDIDE

Be happy, my friend. You deserve it.
(PANGLOSS *hurries back to the table, delighted.*)

DUKE OF NAPLES

(*At table*)
I place the Duchy of Naples on number four.

FERONE

Your pardon, my Duke. But Naples belongs to your mother.

DUKE OF NAPLES

My mother died at dinner. Or if she didn't, she will die at
breakfast.

PANGLOSS

My goodness! What a way to speak of your mother.

DUKE OF NAPLES

(*To* PANGLOSS)

Lend me five thousand. You must come and spend Easter with us.

PANGLOSS

(*Gives him money*)

How kind of you.

FERONE

The Duchy of Naples to be covered.

SULTAN

(*To the* MARQUIS, *as they bump into* CANDIDE)

I have seen that man before.

MARQUIS

And I. But I can't remember where. In any case, it is a pleasant picture that comes down memory's lane.

(CANDIDE *stands staring at them, but they move away*.)

CROUPIER

Number five wins again.

DUKE OF NAPLES

(*To* PANGLOSS)

My dear friend, lend me another ten thousand.

PANGLOSS

With pleasure. What a charming game this is! I now have thousands of lire and wish to place it all on number five. Then I'll buy cakes for everybody.

FERONE

(*To* SOFRONIA)

This gentleman is in search of a lady. Will you help him, Madame Sofronia?

SOFRONIA

(*Who is masked, to* CANDIDE *who is masked*)

I certainly will. (*She pushes* CANDIDE *into bedroom*) You got troubles? You should know about me. You got a mother and a father? (*Before he can answer*) You got uncles? No? So you got no troubles.

(OLD LADY *sings, to the music of a gavotte*)

I've got troubles, as I said.
Mother's dying, Father's dead.
All my uncles are in jail.

(CANDIDE *sings*)

It's a very moving tale.

(CUNEGONDE, *wearing mask, enters with coffee tray.*)

(SOFRONIA *continues singing*)

Though our name, I say again, is
Quite the proudest name in Venice,

Our afflictions are so many,
And we haven't got a penny.

(CANDIDE *sings*)

Madam, I am desolate
At your family's tragic state
Any help that I can give . . .
Please do tell me where they live.

I shall look them up tomorrow
And alleviate their sorrow
With a check made out to bearer.
In the meantime, buona sera.

(SOFRONIA *sings*)

I've got troubles, as I said
Mother's dying, Father's dead.
All my uncles are in jail.

(CANDIDE *sings*)

It's a very moving tale.

(SOFRONIA *sings*)

Although our name, I say again, is
Quite the proudest name in Venice,
All my uncles are in jail.

(SOFRONIA *and* CANDIDE *sing*)

It's a very moving tale.
Ah, what a moving tale!

(*Outside, in the gambling room,* PANGLOSS *is being generous to the pretty ladies.*)

CANDIDE

(PANGLOSS *sings*)

Millions of rubles and lire and francs¹
Broke the bank, broke the bank.
Broke the best of all possible banks.
Pieces of gold to the ladies I throw.
Easy come, easy go.
Shining gold to the ladies I throw.

See them on their knees before me.
If they love me, can you blame them?
Little wonder they adore me.
Watch them woo me as I name them:

(*As he names each lady he gives her gold coins*)
Lady Frilly, Lady Silly,
Pretty Lady Willy-Nilly,
Lady Lightly, Lady Brightly,
Charming Lady Fly-by-Nightly.

My Lady Fortune found me.
What a joy to have around me
Lovely ladies, six or seven.
This is my idea of Heaven.

Fortune, keep the wheel a-spinning, spinning,
They adore me while I'm winning!

Lady Frilly, Lady Silly,
Pretty Lady Willy-Nilly,
Lady Lightly, Lady Brightly,
Charming Lady Fly-by-Nightly.

Fools love only one or two,
Ladies, I love all of you.

(OLD LADY *and*
CUNEGONDE *in bed-
room*)

I've got troubles, as I
said.
Mother is dying, Fa-
ther's dead
All my uncles are in jail

(CANDIDE *in bed-
room*)

It's a very moving tale.

(OLD LADY *and*
CUNEGONDE)

Although our name, I
say again, is
Quite the proudest
name in Venice,
All my uncles are in jail.

(OLD LADY, CUNE-
GONDE *and* CANDIDE)

It's a very moving
tale . . .

(PANGLOSS)

Lady Frilly, Lady Silly,
Pretty Lady Willy-
Nilly,
Lady Lightly, Lady
Brightly,
Charming Lady Fly-by-
Nightly.

My Lady Fortune
found me
What a joy to have
around me
Lovely ladies, six or
seven.
This is my idea of
Heaven.
Fortune, keep the wheel
a-spinning, spinning,
They adore me while
I'm winning!

(PANGLOSS *and* TALL
GIRLS)

Lady Frilly, Lady Silly,
Pretty Lady Willy-
Nilly,
Lady Lightly, Lady
Brightly,

*Simul-
taneously*

130

Charming Lady Fly-by-
Nightly.

(CUNEGONDE, OLD
LADY *and* CANDIDE)
She's got troubles ...

Fools love only one or
two,
Ladies, I love all of you.

*Simul-
taneously*

(*In the bedroom,* CANDIDE, *his back to the wall, is pinned down by* CUNEGONDE *and* SOFRONIA. *He tries to move, but he is a prisoner.* SOFRONIA *turns* CANDIDE *about and* CUNEGONDE *tries to snip off his bags of gold. The try is not successful. But* CUNEGONDE *and* SOFRONIA *are determined, and caution is thrown to the winds.* CANDIDE *moves to the now empty gambling room and is pursued by* CUNEGONDE *and* SOFRONIA. *In the scuffle, the masks are knocked off.* CANDIDE, CUNEGONDE *and* SOFRONIA *stand staring at each other.*)

CANDIDE

(*Very softly*)

Cunegonde. (*He turns to stare at* SOFRONIA, *then turns back to stare at* CUNEGONDE) My pretty, my sweet, my pure Cunegonde. My whole life has gone trying to find you. And so I've found you. (*Takes off the bags of gold and throws them down*) This is what you want. I give it to you.

(*He crosses room, and exits.* FERONE *enters, picks up bags, looks at* CUNEGONDE. *She is crying.*)

FERONE

You are fools, both of you. The game is to get what you want without the man knowing you got it. He will go to the police. ...

CUNEGONDE

(*Sadly*)

No. This man won't go to the police.

FERONE

(*To* SOFRONIA)

Get out. You're not worth your supper. Get out.

PANGLOSS

(*Comes into the empty gambling room*)

Now where has everybody gone? Hello, Cunegonde. Oh, dear child, how you have changed. (*Peers at* CUNEGONDE. *She exits. He speaks to* SOFRONIA) Oh, madame. A most disturbing series of events has come my way. I was standing with my arms full of money. I was robbed. And now the gaming table has strangely disappeared—

SOFRONIA

(*Wearily*)

Yes. It's all moved to another room. And you will not be admitted. (*Bitterly*) Be smart. Come back tomorrow night and try again.

(*She exits.*)

PANGLOSS

But I loaned a lot of money to a nice gentleman and a lady.... Oh, I am sure they are looking for me now. (*Calling out*) Gentlemen. This is Dr. Pangloss. I'm in here. Could you return the money now? (*Long pause. Sadly*) I'll wait. I'm sure they are looking for me.

(*The lights dim as Venice moves off and Westphalia comes into place.*)

SCENE 3

The Scene: Westphalia in ruins.
At rise: MAXIMILLIAN *is on stage alone.* CANDIDE, CUNEGONDE,
OLD LADY *and* PANGLOSS *come in. They do not see* MAXIMILLIAN.

PANGLOSS

(*To* CUNEGONDE, *who looks around and starts to cry*)
Now, now. The place doesn't look very nice, but there's always something homey about coming home.

MAXIMILLIAN

Well, look who's come home. Cunegonde. My God, you're ugly.

CUNEGONDE

My own brother. Deserted me—you deserted me in Buenos Aires. What are you doing here?

MAXIMILLIAN

Resting. I didn't desert you in Buenos Aires. (*Points to* CANDIDE) *He* killed me.

OLD LADY

(*To* CANDIDE)
What's the matter with you, you can't even kill a man?

133

MAXIMILLIAN

(*To* CUNEGONDE)

Your lover killed me—

CUNEGONDE

He's not my lover. How dare you talk such filth? Never been my lover—

OLD LADY

Once they were going to give a medal to a man who hadn't been your lover. They looked and looked—

(CUNEGONDE *swipes at the* OLD LADY.)

CUNEGONDE

(*Peers at* MAXIMILLIAN)

What did you do with your teeth?

MAXIMILLIAN

Sold them. I had many an adventure, I can tell you—

CUNEGONDE

Don't tell me. A man who would sell his teeth would sell his sister. (*Shouts to Heaven*) Our sainted mother knows that you sold your own sister. (*Shrieks*) Mother, look down at your son and make him give me the money—

MAXIMILLIAN

(*To* PANGLOSS, *pointing to* CUNEGONDE *and* CANDIDE)

Have they both gone crazy?

PANGLOSS

Candide has not spoken these many weeks. I think he's a little upset.

CUNEGONDE

I've come home to die. (*Nobody answers*) I think I'm dying.

OLD LADY

So die.

MAXIMILLIAN

Dig me a little grave, sister. I'm so tired.

CUNEGONDE

I'll make you curses. You stole my fortune, tore the pearls from our mother's breast and gave them to women—

OLD LADY

Really? I never would have guessed that.

CUNEGONDE

Bring me a winding sheet.

OLD LADY

Don't be so modest.

PANGLOSS

I want only to cover my head. A head that was honored by Heidelberg should not be injured by the damp. I should, of course, like a stone over my grave, and one word—teacher— carved thereon. Then, in smaller letters, add that the deceased had nine degrees, three of them doctorates in—

CANDIDE

(*Quietly*)

In lies. You were my master, and I loved you, and you taught me lies. I was a stupid boy, and you must have known it. (*With great force*) A man should be jailed for telling lies to the young.

PANGLOSS

(*Shocked*)

Candide.

CANDIDE

Go away and lie to the trees.

PANGLOSS

Candide.

CANDIDE

You are a useless old man. Go away from here.
(PANGLOSS *goes slowly off.*)

MAXIMILLIAN

(*To* CANDIDE)

You are ill-born. Nobody but the ill-born would speak that way to a man older than himself.

CANDIDE

I killed you once. A man could grow to like killing you. So get out before I do it again.
(*Frightened,* MAXIMILLIAN *moves off.*)

136

OLD LADY

Glad he's gone. Never did a day's work in his life.

CANDIDE

And did you?
(*He begins to make a fire.*)

OLD LADY

Are you making a fire?

CANDIDE

Yes.

OLD LADY

What are you going to cook?

CANDIDE

Nothing for you. You'll get along. You always have. But not here. Get out.

OLD LADY

I've told you what happened to me. I've told you of my past—

CANDIDE

Yes, you had trouble. And so you lived on the world. I'm sick of your past—and mine. Get out.
(*She goes slowly off.*)

CUNEGONDE

I'm hungry.

CANDIDE

So am I.

CUNEGONDE

I'm a woman—

CANDIDE

Do they get hungrier than men? (*Smiles*) Yes they do. In that fairy tale we lived in.

CUNEGONDE

I feel so tired—

CANDIDE

I followed you around the world, believing every foolish tale you told me, killing men for something called your honor.

CUNEGONDE

I was alone, I was frightened. I—

CANDIDE

Yes, I think that's true. I don't blame you, Cunegonde. My head was full of nonsense. But now I am tired of nonsense. I want to live. So go away and let me live.

(CUNEGONDE *rises and goes slowly off.* PANGLOSS *comes in. He is holding up a fish.*)

PANGLOSS

(*Timidly, to* CANDIDE)

I just came back for a minute. I brought you a little fish. I took a short course in oceanography at Leipzig. I used to be good at such things. Did you ever know that?

CANDIDE

I never knew you were good at anything.

PANGLOSS

I think I could summon back a little knowledge of . . . er . . . of the common-life things, if I tried. . . .

CANDIDE

Try hard.

PANGLOSS

You see . . . er . . . well . . . I was early taught in life that everything was for the best in this best of all possible worlds. I don't think I ever believed it, but it's most difficult to get rid of what you once thought, isn't it?

CANDIDE

(*Puts a pot on the fire*)
Most difficult. But let's not philosophize about not philosophizing. Let's make a place to sleep.
(*The* OLD LADY *and* MAXIMILLIAN *come in. She is bowed down under twigs and branches and looks like a forest moving.* MAXIMILLIAN *is carrying a homemade broom.*)

MAXIMILLIAN

I never carried anything before.

CANDIDE

(*To* MAXIMILLIAN)
What are you doing here?

OLD LADY

(*Hastily*)

He's going to work hard. He's promised me. You can't put him out. He'll die. He's so silly. And anyway, I've always wanted a son. (MAXIMILLIAN *is sweeping the air with the broom. She hits him*) The air ain't dirty. Sweep the ground. (*Hastily, to* CANDIDE) I've got wood for a fire, and dandelions and fiddle-heads for our dinner. (*Points at* PANGLOSS, *who is having a bad time cleaning the fish*) Look who is doing what all wrong.

CANDIDE

Go to work and mind your business.

OLD LADY

I'm going to make us all some sensible shoes. If you're born a princess as I was, of course, your feet always hurt. Even through war and rape and ...

(CANDIDE *stares at her. She is silent.* CUNEGONDE *enters. There are leaves in her hair and she is clean. She has done her best to be pretty again.*)

CUNEGONDE

(*She is carrying a giant mushroom, timidly*)

I brought something for our dinner. I'm clean. (*Nobody answers. She throws the mushroom into the pot*) Mushrooms are good in a stew.

OLD LADY

(*Hauling the mushroom out of the stew, shrieking*)

It's a poison mushroom, you silly woman. This is not the last supper. Can't you do anything in this world except get other people in trouble?

CUNEGONDE
(*Timidly*)

Yes. I can cook. . . . (*She goes to the stew pot, stirs it, knocks it over. She sinks on the ground in shame*) She's right. There's nothing I can do. Nothing.

CANDIDE
(*Smiles*)

Still boasting, aren't you? (*He comes to her*) Marry me, Cunegonde.

CUNEGONDE
(*Sadly, softly*)

It's too late. I'm not young, I'm not good, I'm not pure.

CANDIDE

And I am not young, and not worth much. What we wanted, we will not have. The way we did love, we will not love again. Come now, let us take what we have and love as we are.

PANGLOSS

I'd love to do a ceremony. I had three weeks of divinity school in the Würzburg Gymnasium. Now you must say after me, "Love between men and women is the highest order of love between men and women. Thus we promise to think noble and do noble. . . ."

CANDIDE
(*With force*)

No. We will not think noble because we are not noble. We will not live in beautiful harmony because there is no such thing in this world, nor should there be. We promise only to do our best and live out our lives. Dear God, that's all we can promise in truth. Marry me, Cunegonde.

(CANDIDE *sings*)

You've been a fool and so have I,
But come and be my wife,
And let us try before we die
To make some sense of life.
We're neither pure nor wise nor good;
We'll do the best we know;
We'll build our house, and chop our wood,
And make our garden grow.
And make our garden grow.

(CUNEGONDE *sings*)

I thought the world was sugar-cake,
For so our master said;
But now I'll teach my hands to bake
Our loaf of daily bread.

(CANDIDE *and* CUNEGONDE *sing*)

We're neither pure nor wise nor good;
We'll do the best we know;
We'll build our house, and chop our wood,
And make our garden grow.
And make our garden grow.

(*Cast begins slow entry. Sextette of* PANGLOSS, MAXIMIL-
LIAN, OLD LADY, CUNEGONDE, CANDIDE *and* GOVERNOR *sing*)

Let dreamers dream what worlds they please;
Those Edens can't be found.

The sweetest flowers, the fairest trees
Are grown in solid ground.

(*Entire company sings*)
We're neither pure nor wise nor good.
We'll do the best we know.
We'll build our house, and chop our wood,
And make our garden grow.
And make our garden grow.

Curtain